volume fourteen of
the illustrated history of movies through posters

Images from the Hershenson-Allen Archive

Previous Volumes:
Volume One: Cartoon Movie Posters
Volume Two: Cowboy Movie Posters
Volume Three: Academy Award® Winners' Movie Posters
Volume Four: Sports Movie Posters
Volume Five: Crime Movie Posters
Volume Six: More Cowboy Movie Posters
Volume Seven: Horror Movie Posters
Volume Eight: Best Pictures' Movie Posters
Volume Nine: Musical Movie Posters
Volume Ten: Serial Movie Posters
Volume Eleven: Horror, Sci-Fi & Fantasy Movie Posters
Volume Twelve: Comedy Movie Posters
Volume Thirteen: War Movie Posters

Edited by Richard Allen and Bruce Hershenson
Published by Bruce Hershenson
P.O. Box 874, West Plains, MO 65775
Phone: (417) 256-9616 Fax: (417) 257-6948
mail@brucehershenson.com (e-mail)
http://www.brucehershenson.com or
http://www.emovieposter.com (website)

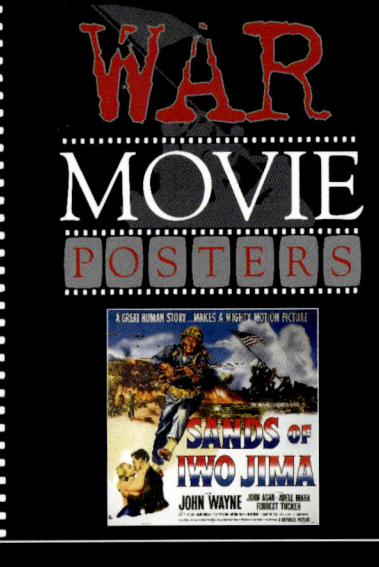

IF YOU ENJOYED THIS MOVIE POSTER BOOK, THEN YOU ARE SURE TO ENJOY THESE OTHER SIMILAR BRUCE HERSHENSON PUBLICATIONS. LOOK FOR THEM AT YOUR LOCAL BOOKSTORE OR ORDER THEM DIRECT FROM THE PUBLISHER. ORDER YOUR COPY OF **WAR MOVIE POSTERS** TODAY!

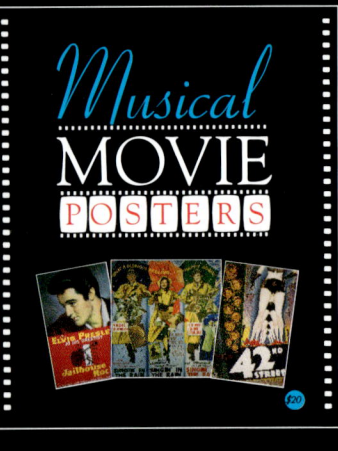
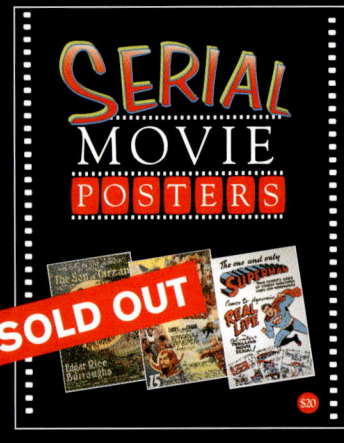

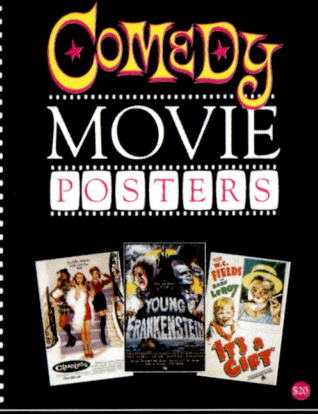

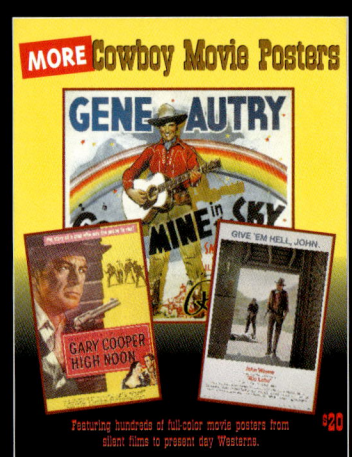

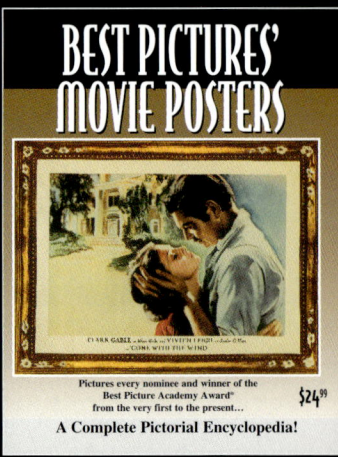
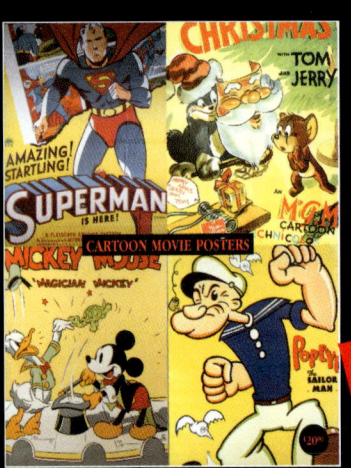

INTRODUCTION

Welcome to the fourteenth volume of the Illustrated History of Movies Through Posters. The title of this book, Attack of the "B" Movie Posters, may be confusing to some people. The posters are not primarily from the B-movies (mostly westerns and crime films) of the 1930s and 1940s that occupied the lower halves of double-bills. This kind of B-movie were so-named to distinguish them from the classier films of the day, dubbed A-movies. Rather, the images in this volume are primarily from the low budget type of films that reached their zenith in the 1950s and 1960s at drive-ins across the country (although I have included a selection of posters from before and after this period for historical reference).

I have tried to avoid duplication from my horror and crime books as much as possible, but I felt obliged to rerun some of the best-loved images. I chose the posters solely on the basis of how visually appealing they are (looking for the best art and taglines), as in the vast majority of cases the films themselves range from mediocre to downright dreadful (there are a few better films in this volume, but they are the rare exceptions!).

Some of these posters push the edges of bad taste, both in the realms of sex and violence (and some go way over the edge!). I think it is fair to say that (as the producers of Not Tonite, Henry, #126, so eloquently state) this book is "not recommended if you blush easily"! Of course, times have changed so much (for better or worse) that some of the films that were once "for adults only" would now be rated "PG" and could be shown intact on television!

Of course there have been thousands of films that could qualify for this volume, and I have tried to present an overview of the best of them. But there were many wonderful images I was unable to include due to space limitations, and I plan on doing a sequel in the near future. If a personal favorite film of yours is missing, let me know so I can try to locate a poster from that film (if I don't have it already). And if you have any poster(s) that are not included in this volume that you feel deserve to be, let me know if I can borrow them for use in the sequel.

Unless otherwise noted, the image in this volume is of the original U.S. one-sheet poster (the standard movie poster size, measuring 27" x 41"), from the first release of the film. Other sizes included are lobby cards (11" x 14"), window cards (14" x 22"), inserts (14" x 36"), half-sheets (22" x 28"), three-sheets (41" x 81"), six-sheets (81" x 81"), and foreign posters (varying sizes).

All the images in this book come from the Hershenson-Allen Archive. The archive consists of over 35,000 different movie poster images, all photographed directly from the original posters onto high quality 4" x 5" color transparencies. There is not another resource like it anywhere, and it is the world's foremost source of movie poster images. The Archive has provided images for books, videos, DVDs, magazines, and newspapers.

This is not a catalog of posters for sale, nor do I sell any sort of movie poster reproductions! However, I do sell movie posters of all sorts through public auctions, both "live" and over the Internet. If you are interested in acquiring original vintage movie posters (or any of the other books I have published) visit my website at http://www.brucehershenson.com (the most visited vintage movie poster site on the Internet) or send me a self-addressed stamped envelope for free brochures.

I need to thank Amy Knight who did the layouts and designed the covers for this book, and Courier Graphics, who did the printing. Most of all, I need to thank my partner, Richard Allen. He has always loved movie posters of all years and genres, and he tracked down many of the images in this book. We share a common vision, and we hope to keep publishing these volumes until we have covered every possible genre of film.

I dedicate this book to my best friend, John Sawyer. It was John who many years ago led me to begin searching out these oft-neglected "classic" B-movie posters at a time when almost all collectors were focused on the best of the A-movie posters. Thanks a lot, John!

Bruce Hershenson
December 2000

1. FLAMING YOUTH, 1923, lobby card

2. PITFALLS OF PASSION, 1927, title lobby card

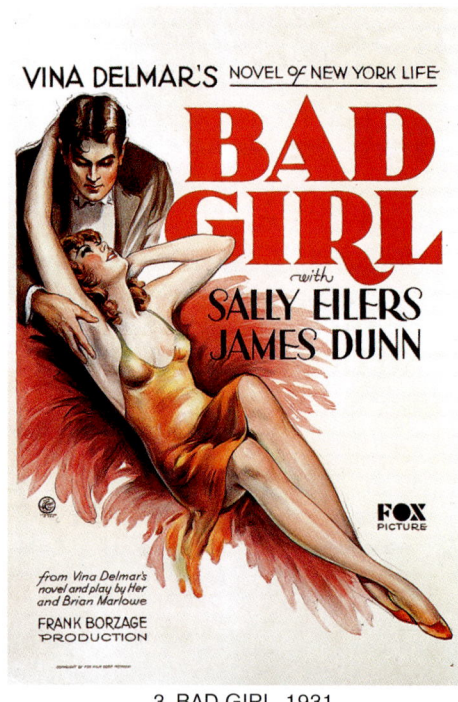

3. BAD GIRL, 1931

4. THE SIN OF NORA MORAN, 1934

5. BORN TO BE BAD, 1934

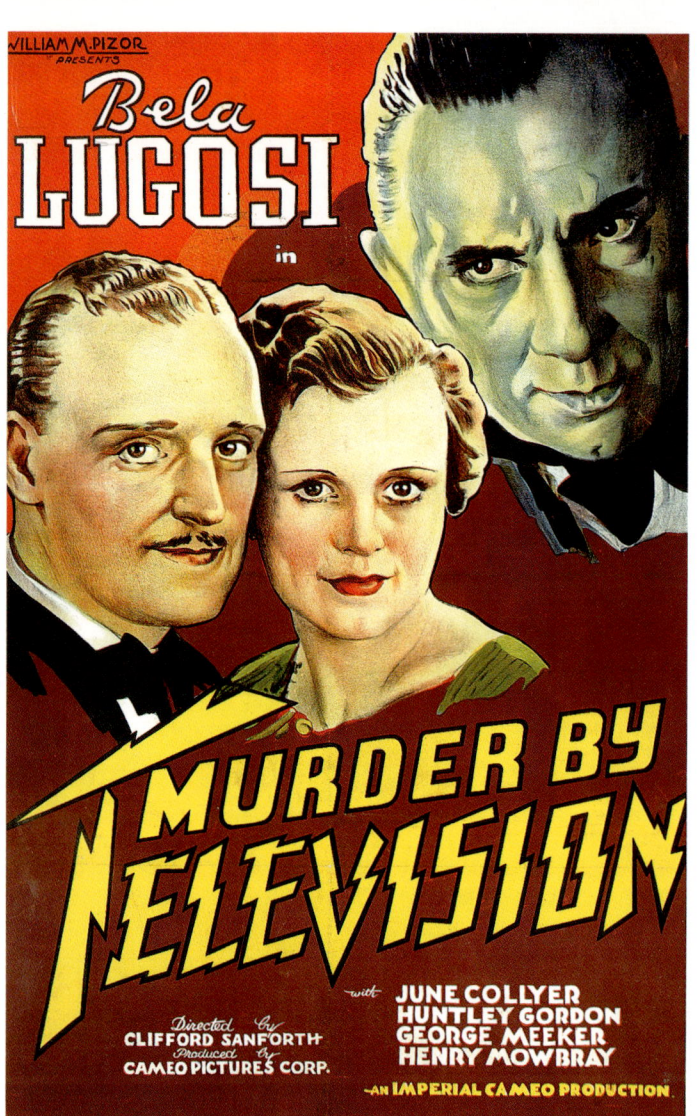

6. MURDER BY TELEVISION, 1935

7. NIGHT WAITRESS, 1936, title lobby card

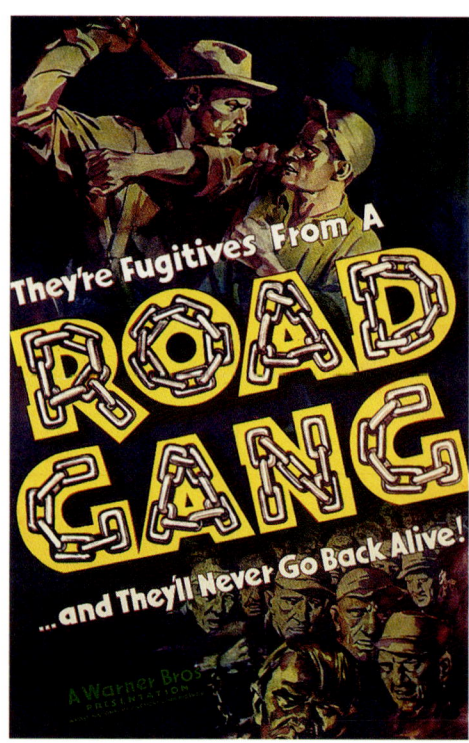

8. ROAD GANG, 1936

9. GAMBLING WITH SOULS, 1936, window card

10. THE LOVE WANGA, 1936

11. THE WAGES OF SIN, 1938

12. PRISON WITHOUT BARS, 1938, title lobby card

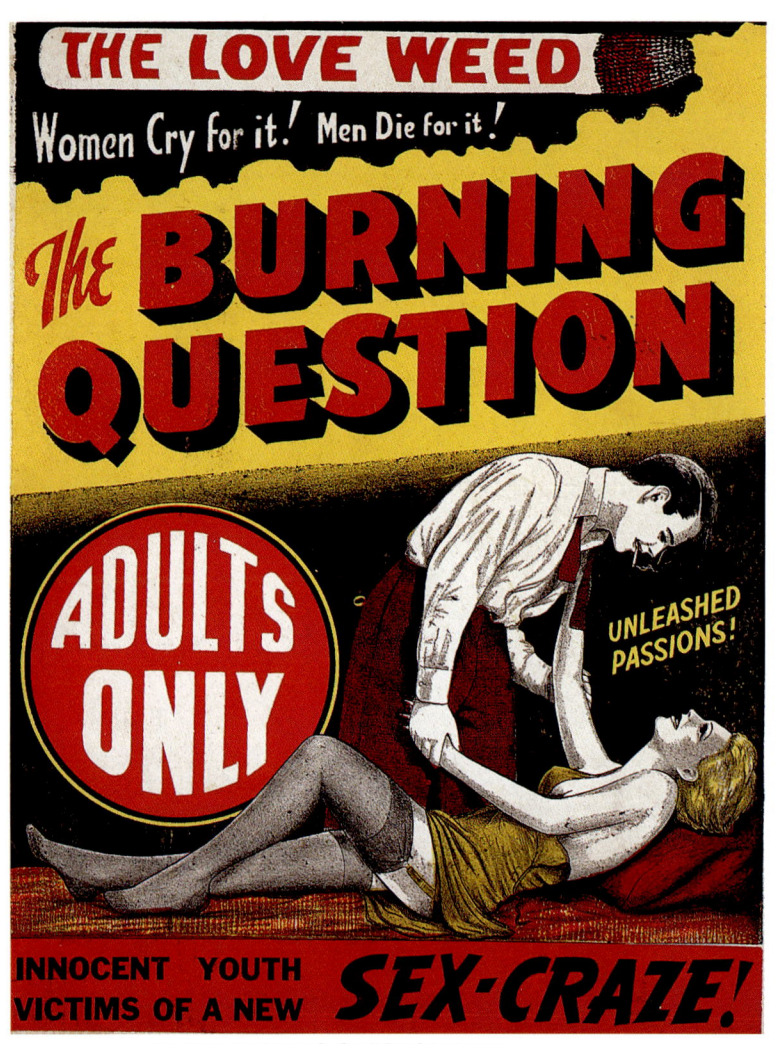
13. THE BURNING QUESTION, 1936, window card

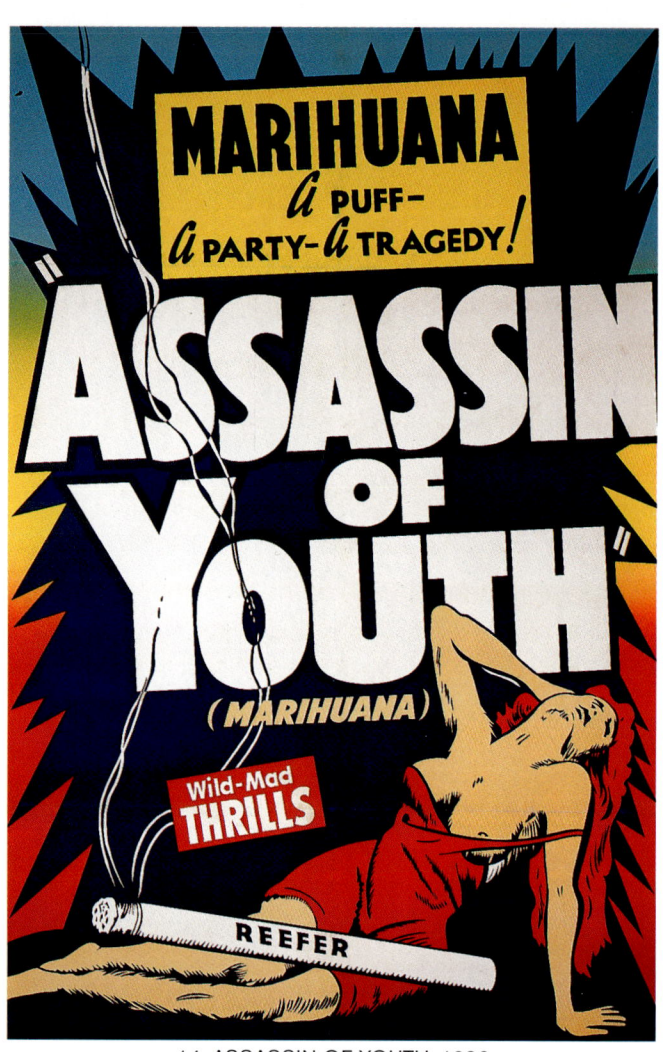
14. ASSASSIN OF YOUTH, 1936

15. MARIHUANA, 1935

16. DEVIL'S HARVEST, 1942

17. DEVIL'S HARVEST, 1942

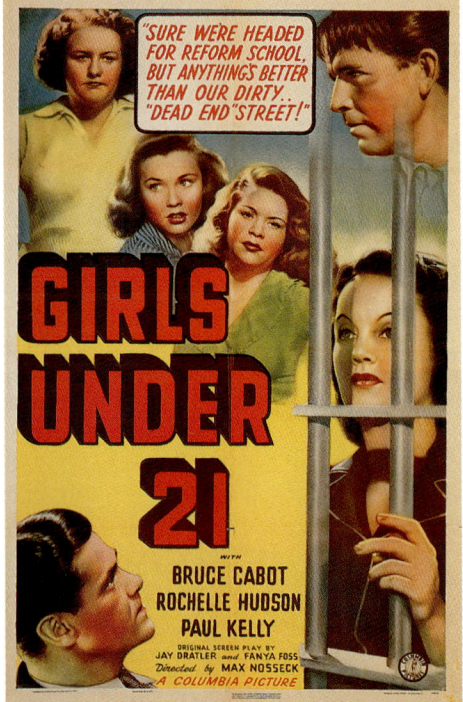

18. NAUGHTY BUT NICE, 1939, half-sheet

19. GIRLS UNDER 21, 1940

20. UNDER AGE, 1941, title lobby card

21. CAPTIVE WILD WOMAN, 1943, title lobby card

22. CHILDREN OF THE WILD, 1940

23. YOUTH RUNS WILD, 1944, title lobby card

24. GIRLS IN CHAINS, 1943

25. TEEN AGE, 1944

26. TEEN AGE, 1944

27. YOUTH AFLAME, 1945

28. WHY GIRLS LEAVE HOME, 1945

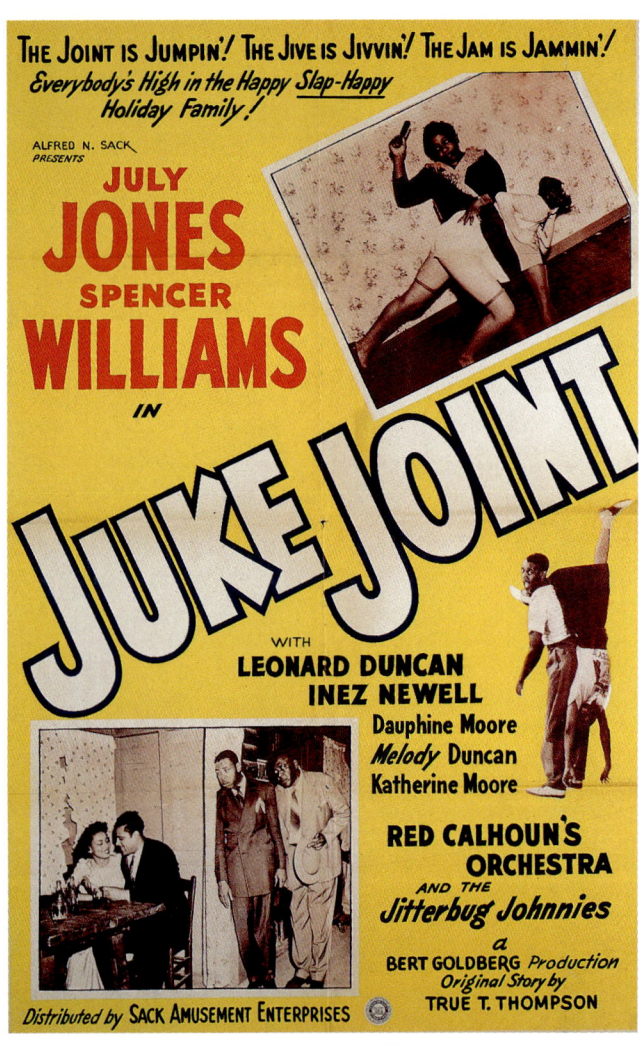

29. JUKE JOINT, 1947

30. SHOULD A GIRL SAY YES?, 1948

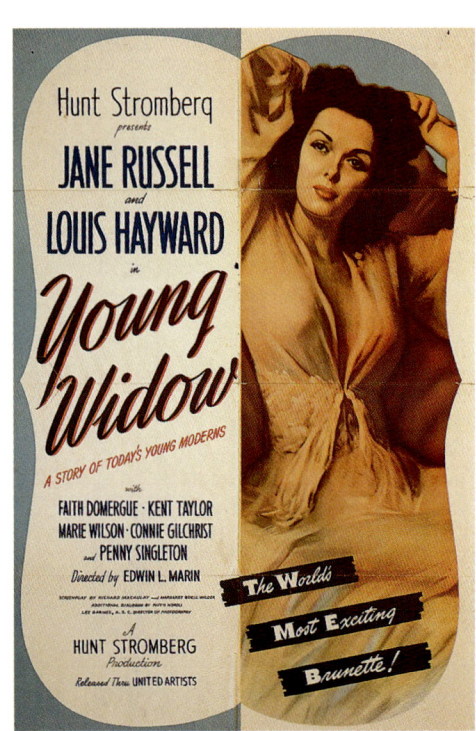

31. YOUNG WIDOW, 1946

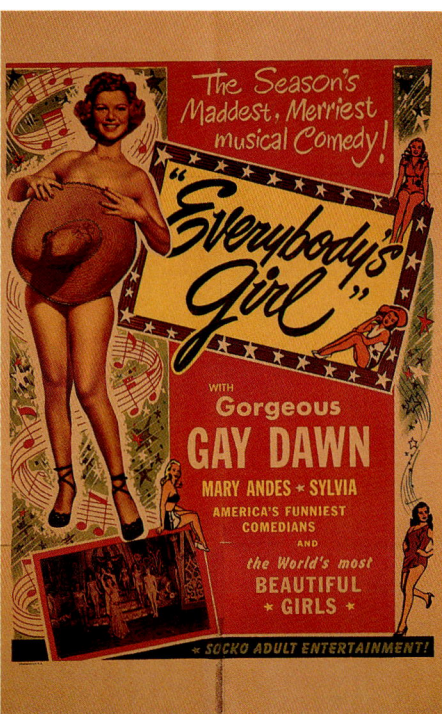

32. EVERYBODY'S GIRL, 1950

33. SO YOUNG, SO BAD, 1950

34. I WALK ALONE, 1948 35. THEY LIVE BY NIGHT, 1949

36. RAMROD, 1947 37. TOO LATE FOR TEARS, 1949 38. ROUGHSHOD, 1949

39. I LOVE TROUBLE, 1948

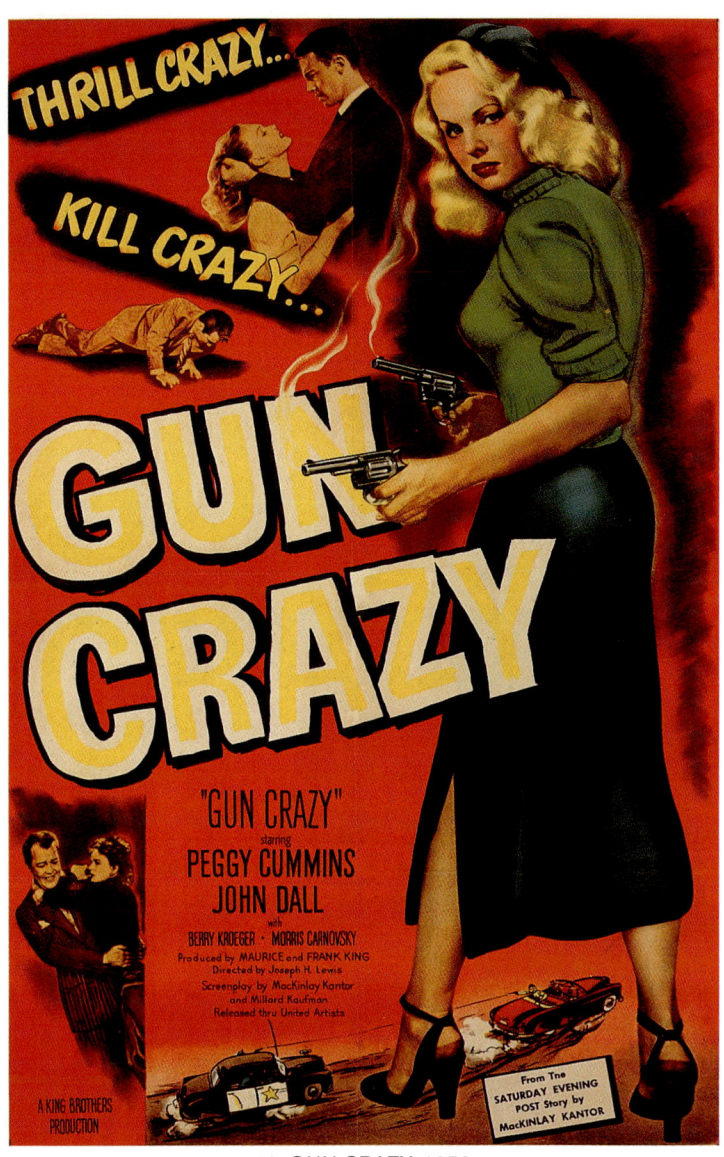
40. GUN CRAZY, 1950

41. KILL OR BE KILLED, 1950

42. I WAS A SHOPLIFTER, 1950, title lobby card

43. PICKUP, 1951

44. THE MAN FROM PLANET X, 1951

45. ROBOT MONSTER, 1953

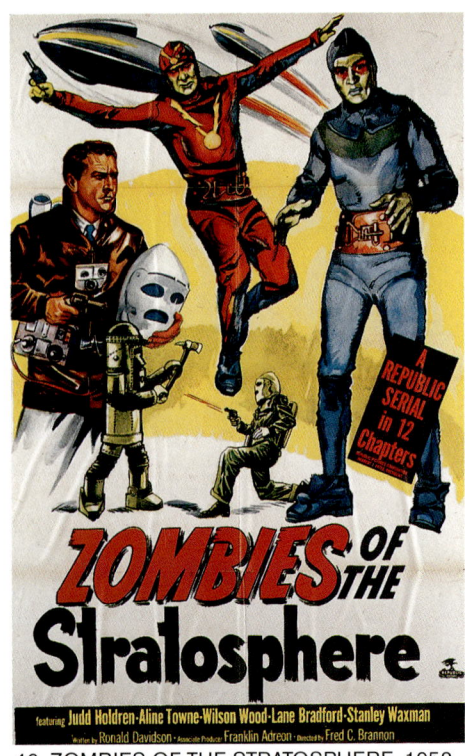

46. ZOMBIES OF THE STRATOSPHERE, 1952

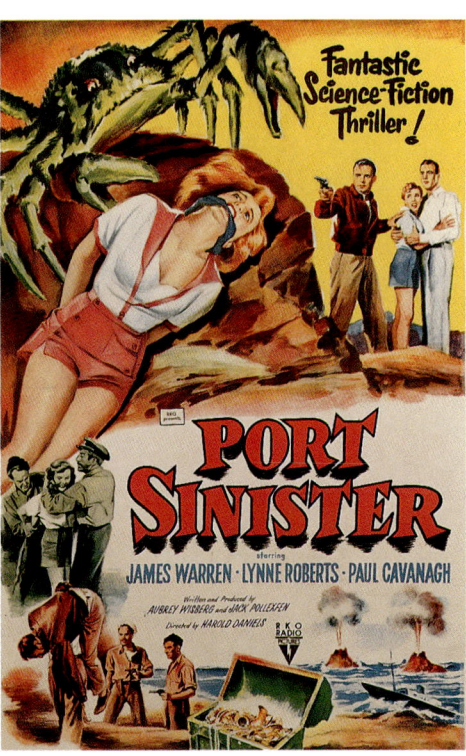

47. PORT SINISTER, 1953

48. MONSTER FROM THE OCEAN FLOOR, 1954

49. CAT-WOMAN OF THE MOON, 1953

50. JUNGLE HEADHUNTERS, 1951

51. BELA LUGOSI MEETS A BROOKLYN GORILLA, 1952

52. UNTAMED MISTRESS, 1953

53. THE NEANDERTHAL MAN, 1953, title lobby card

54. ONE GIRL'S CONFESSION, 1953

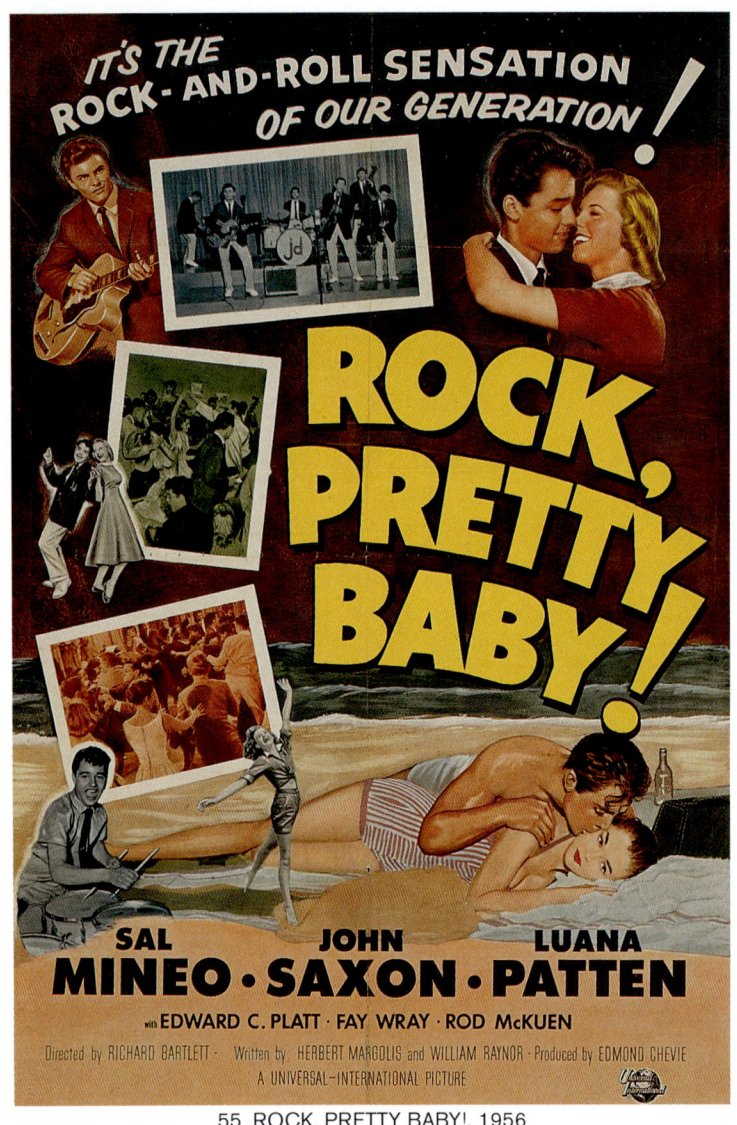
55. ROCK, PRETTY BABY!, 1956

56. ROCK ALL NIGHT, 1957

57. SHAKE, RATTLE AND ROCK!, 1956

58. ROCK, ROCK, ROCK!, 1956, title lobby card

59. FEMALE AND THE FLESH, 1955

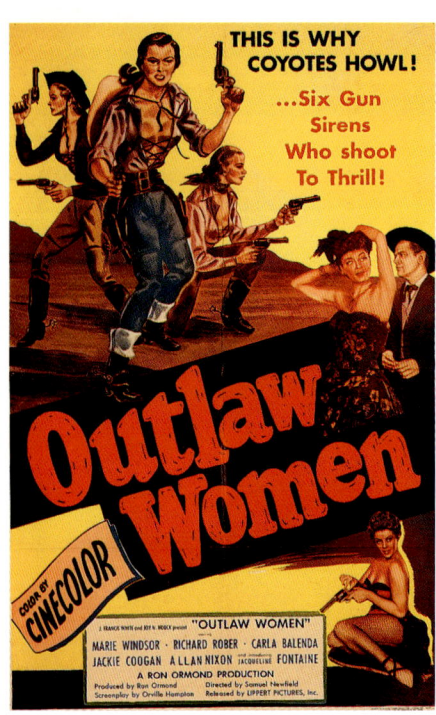
60. OUTLAW WOMEN, 1952

61. JESSE JAMES' WOMEN, 1954

62. THE RESTLESS BREED, 1957

63. SON OF BELLE STARR, 1953

64. THE BUCKSKIN LADY, 1957

65. REFORM SCHOOL GIRL, 1957

66. THE SHE-CREATURE, 1957

67. 20 MILLION MILES TO EARTH, 1957, Danish poster

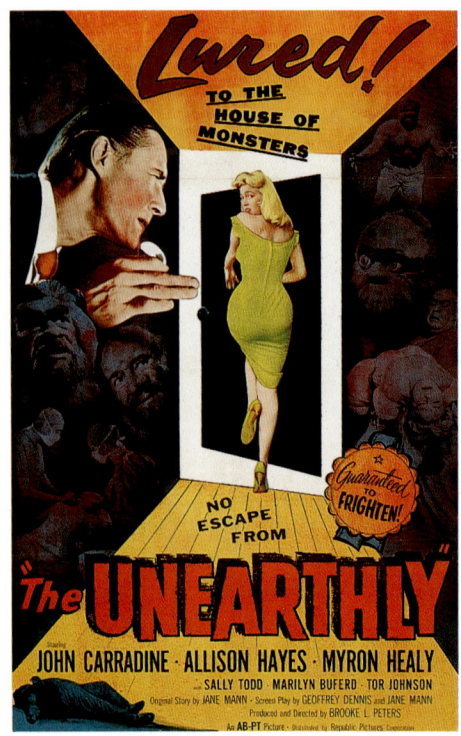

68. THE UNEARTHLY, 1957

69. NOT OF THIS EARTH, 1957, half-sheet

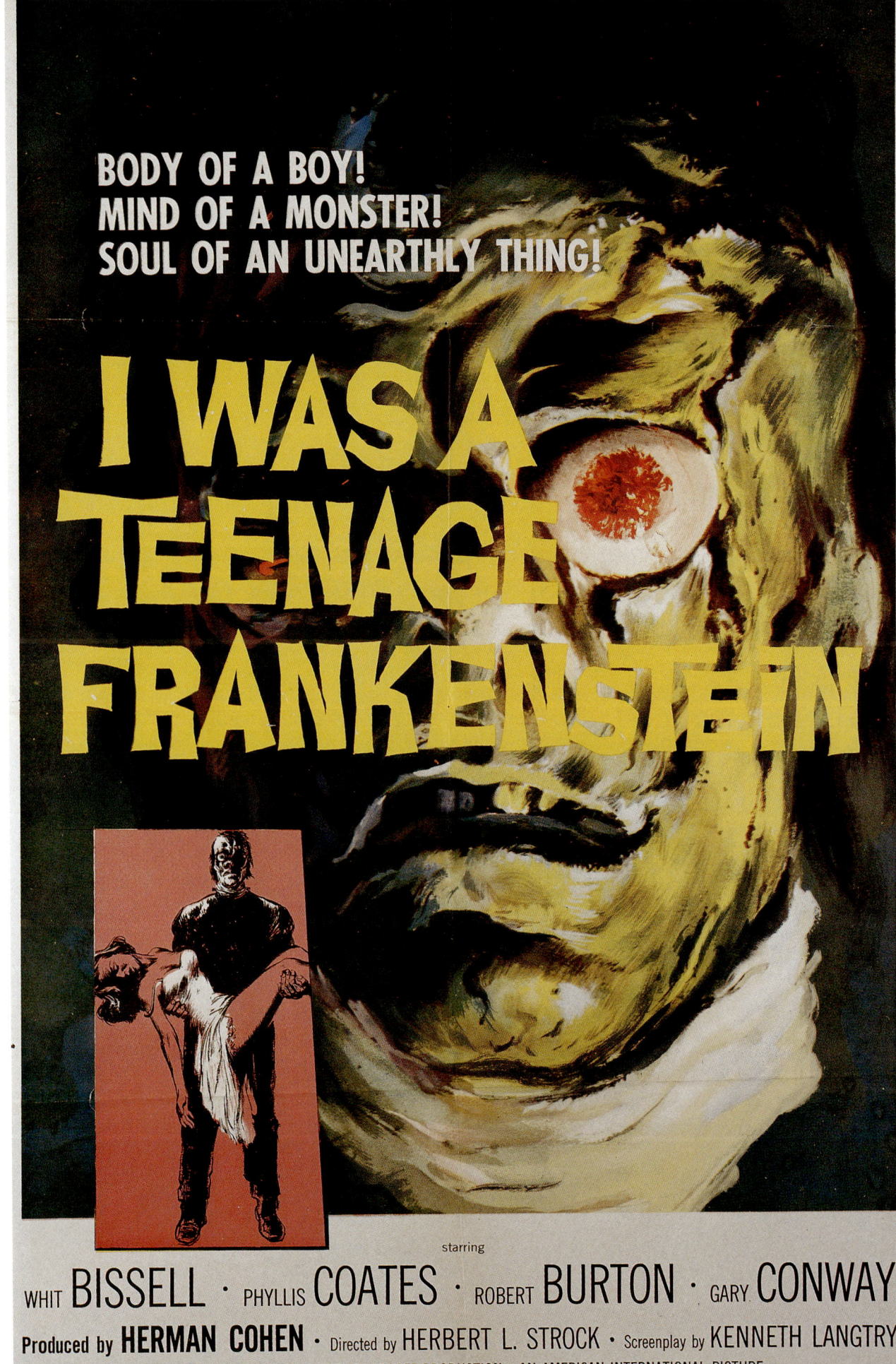

70. I WAS A TEENAGE FRANKENSTEIN, 1957

71. THE NIGHT RUNNER, 1957

72. THE FLESH IS WEAK/BLONDE IN BONDAGE, 1957

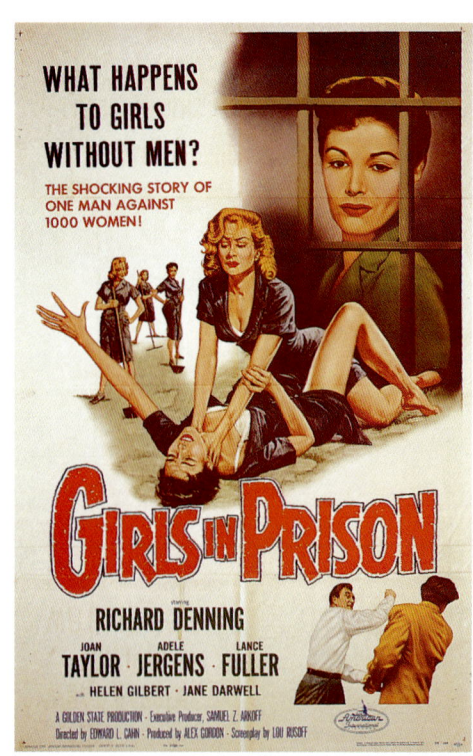

73. GIRLS IN PRISON, 1956

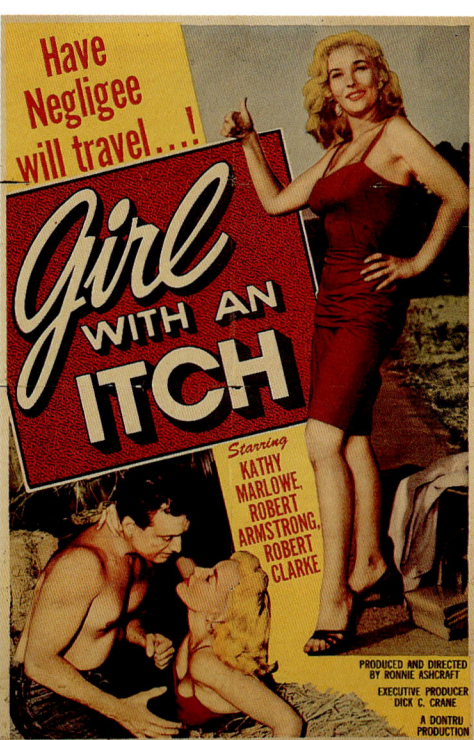

74. GIRL WITH AN ITCH, 1957

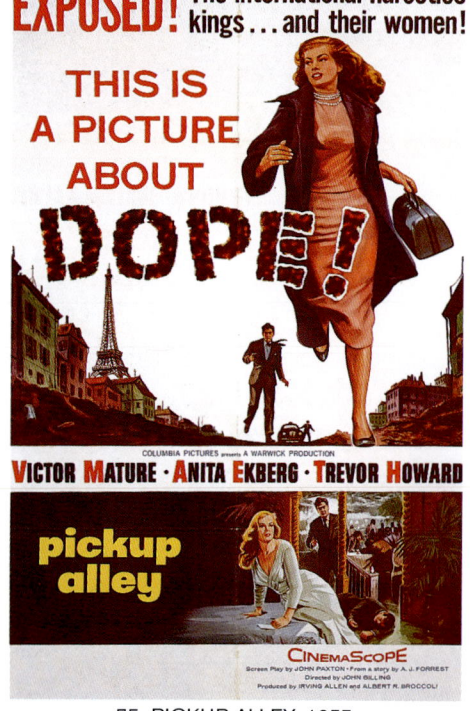

75. PICKUP ALLEY, 1957

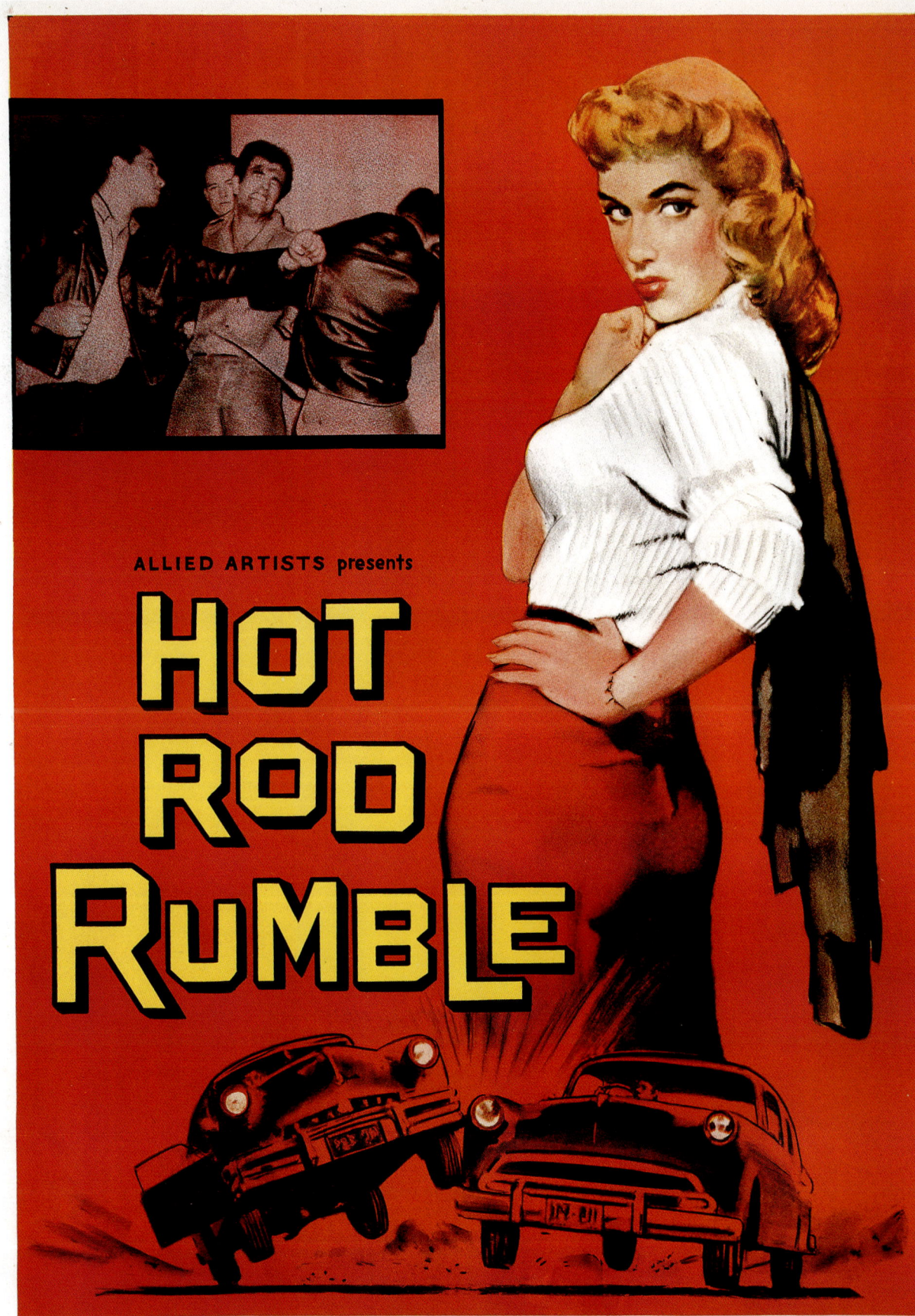

76. HOT ROD RUMBLE, 1957

77. DRAGSTRIP GIRL, 1957

78. HOT CAR GIRL, 1958

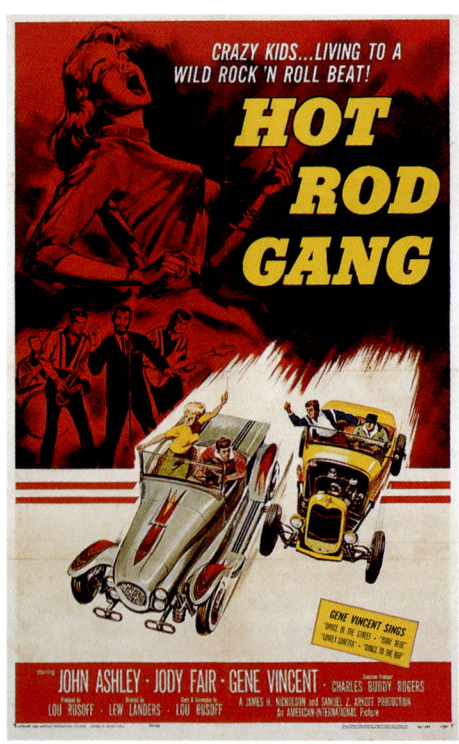

79. HOT ROD GANG, 1958

80. ROAD RACERS, 1958

81. SPEED CRAZY, 1959

82. PLAN 9 FROM OUTER SPACE, 1958

83. THE CAT GIRL, 1957

84. THE CYCLOPS, 1957

85. BACK FROM THE DEAD, 1957

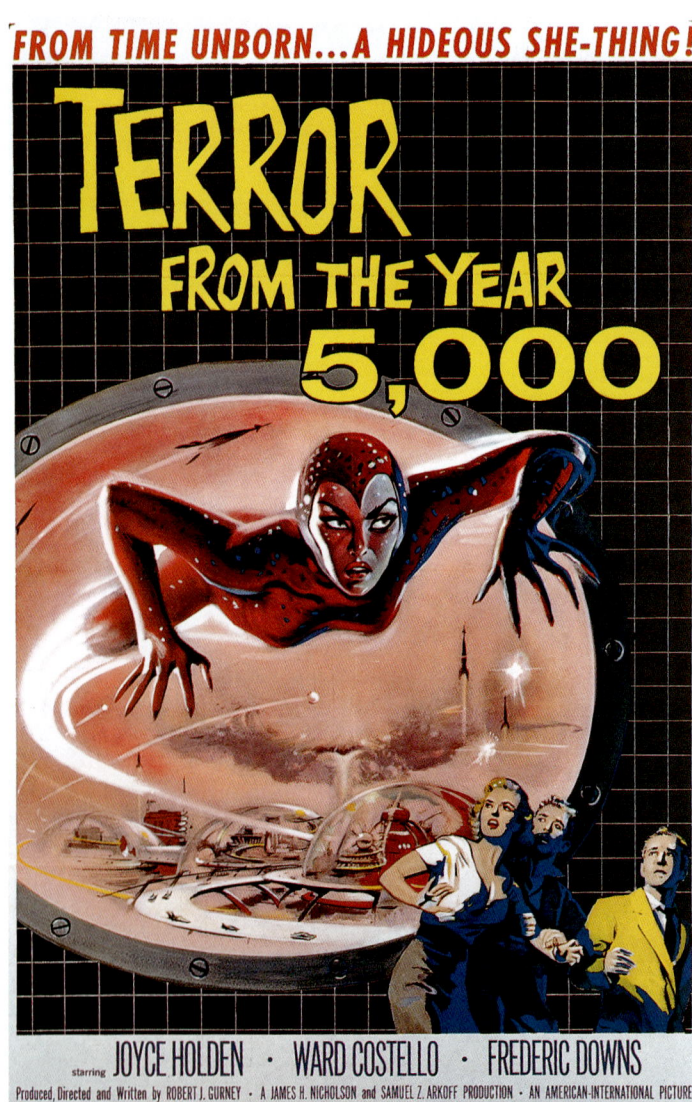
86. TERROR FROM THE YEAR 5,000, 1958

87. SHE DEMONS, 1958

88. FRANKENSTEIN, 1970, 1958

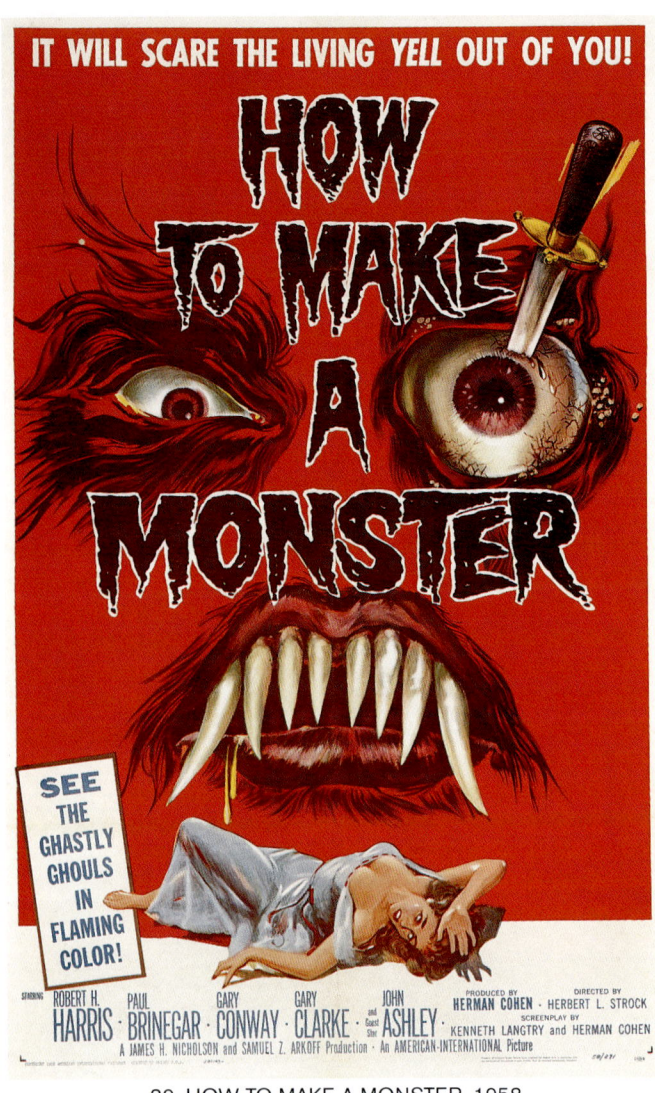
89. HOW TO MAKE A MONSTER, 1958

90. HOUSE ON HAUNTED HILL, 1958, French poster

91. QUEEN OF OUTER SPACE, 1958, Italian poster

92. I BURY THE LIVING, 1958

93. THE BRIDE AND THE BEAST, 1958

94. THE CRAWLING EYE, 1958

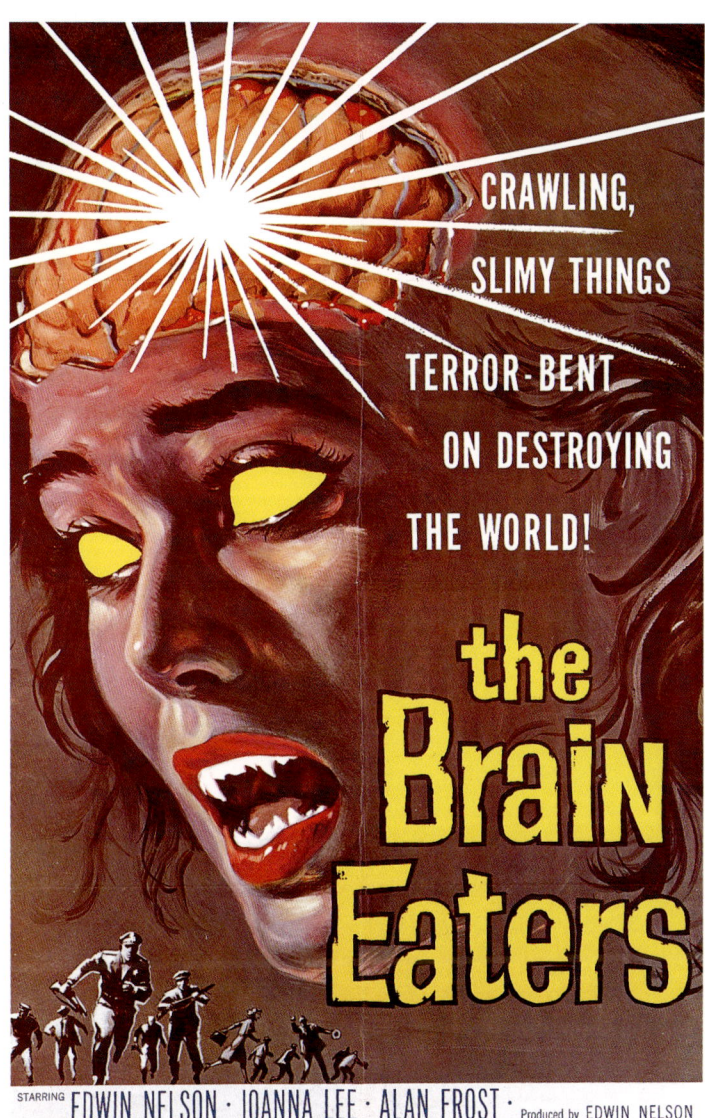
95. THE BRAIN EATERS, 1958

96. THE HAUNTED STRANGLER, 1958

97. RETURN OF THE FLY, 1959

98. HIGH SCHOOL HELLCATS, 1958, half-sheet

99. LOST LONELY AND VICIOUS, 1958

100. HIGH SCHOOL CONFIDENTIAL, 1958, lobby card

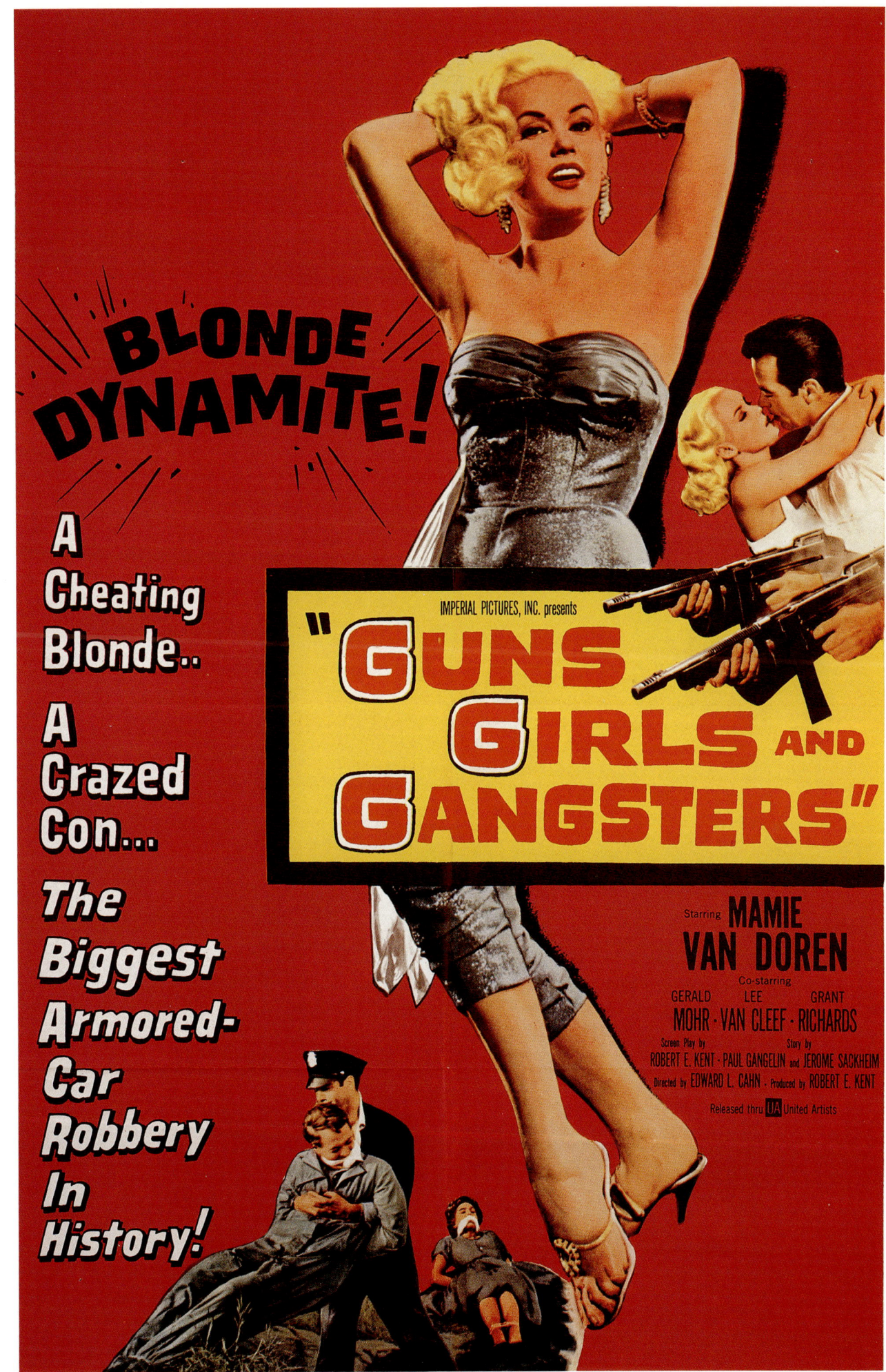

110. GUNS GIRLS AND GANGSTERS, 1959

111. VIRGIN SACRIFICE, 1959

112. PLAYGIRL AFTER DARK, 1959

113. HOT MONEY GIRL, 1959

114. COME DANCE WITH ME!, 1959

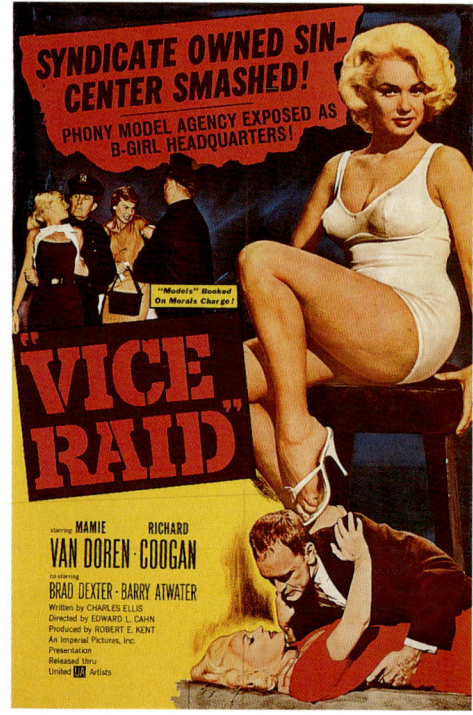
115. VICE RAID, 1959

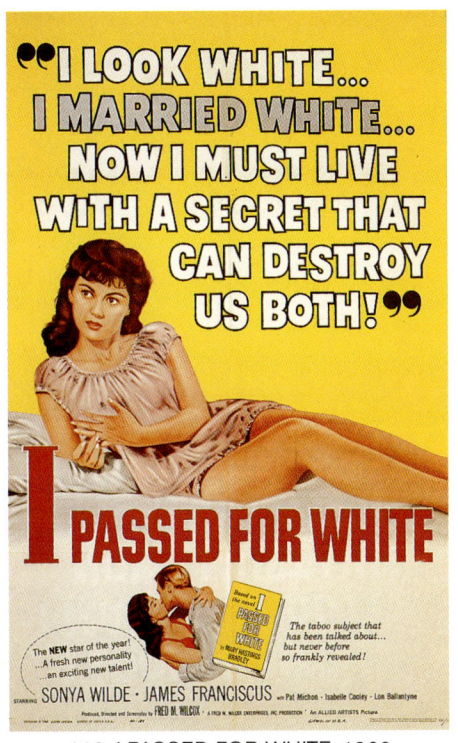

116. I PASSED FOR WHITE, 1960
117. DATE BAIT, 1960
118. BLAZE STARR GOES NUDIST, 1960

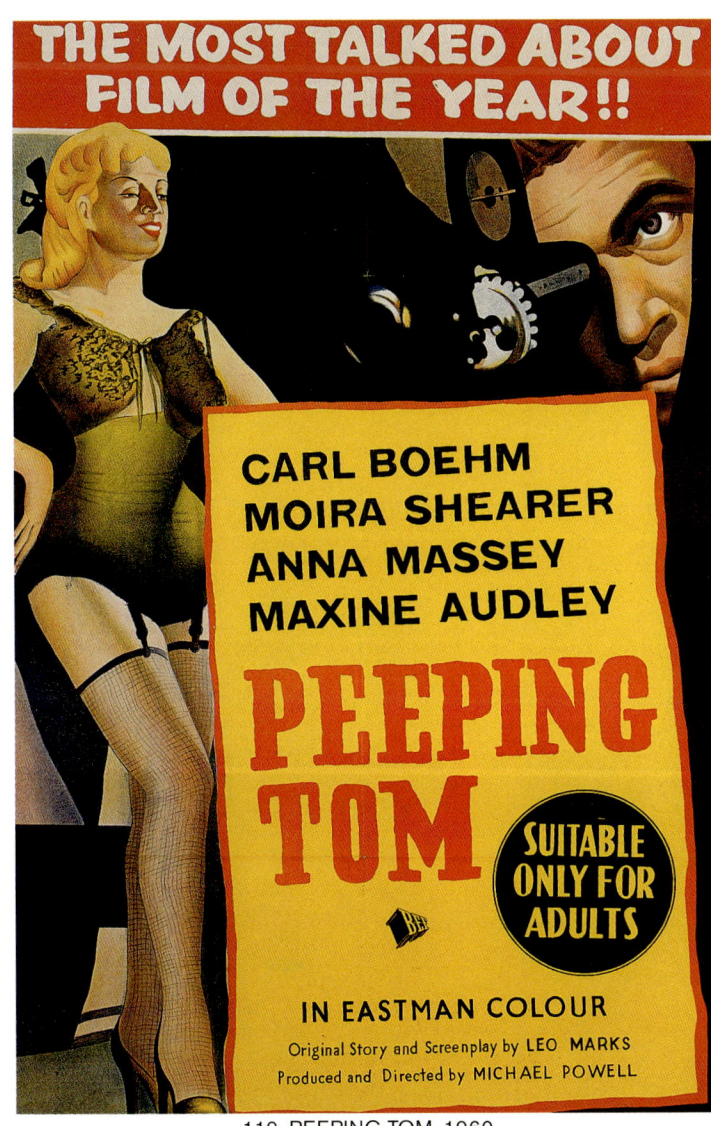
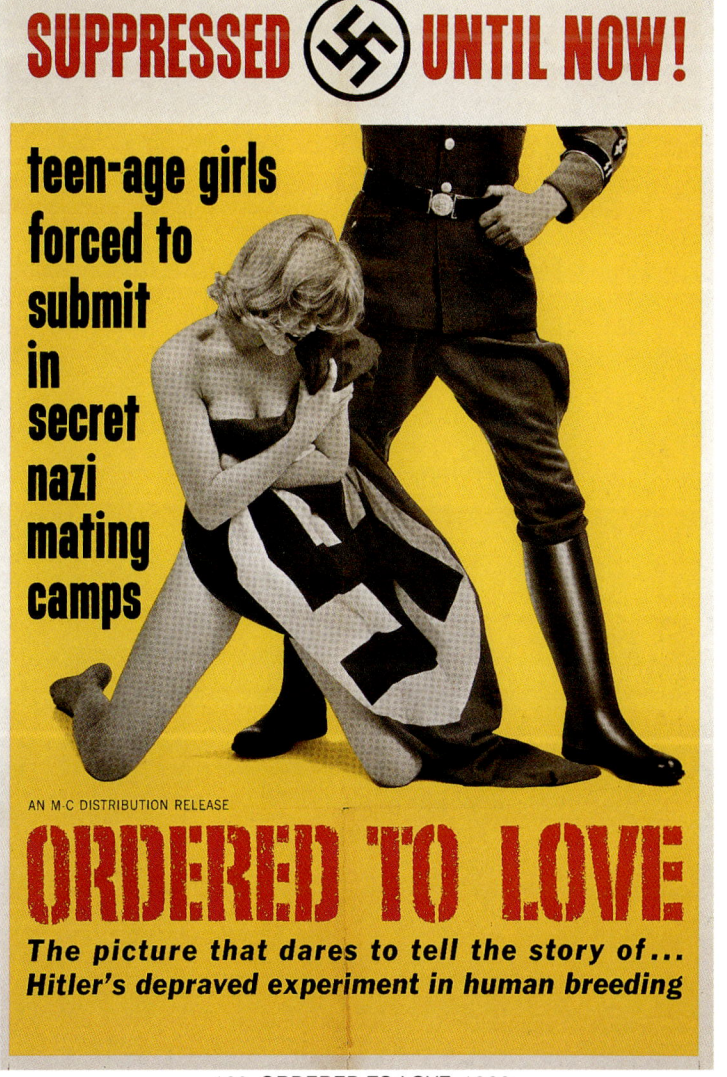

119. PEEPING TOM, 1960
120. ORDERED TO LOVE, 1960

121. TORMENTED, 1960

122. THE LAST WOMAN ON EARTH, 1960

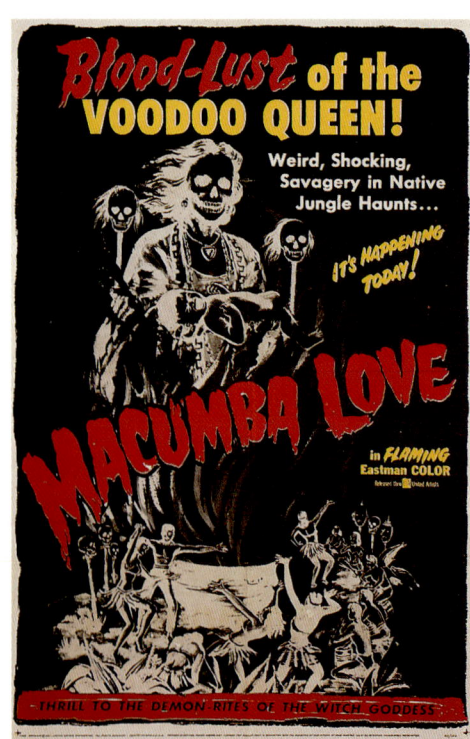
123. MACUMBA LOVE, 1960

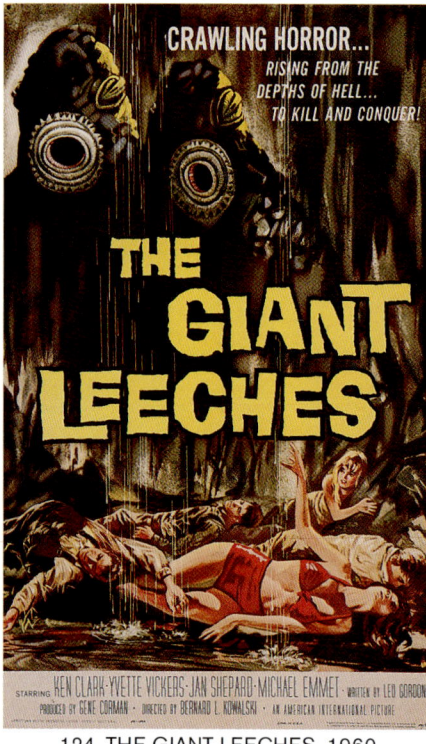
124. THE GIANT LEECHES, 1960

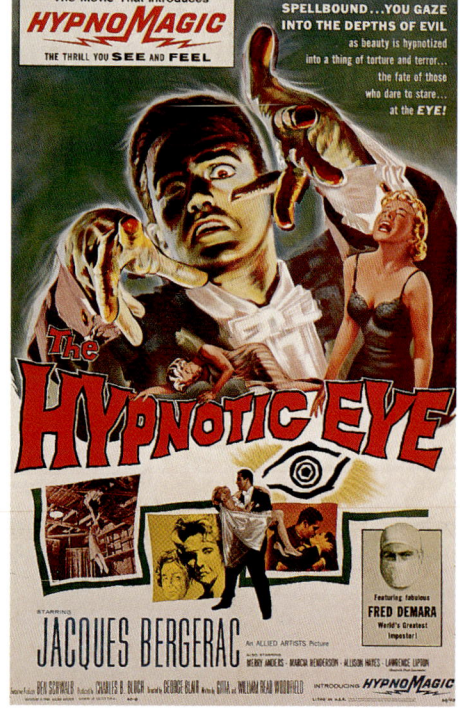
125. THE HYPNOTIC EYE, 1960

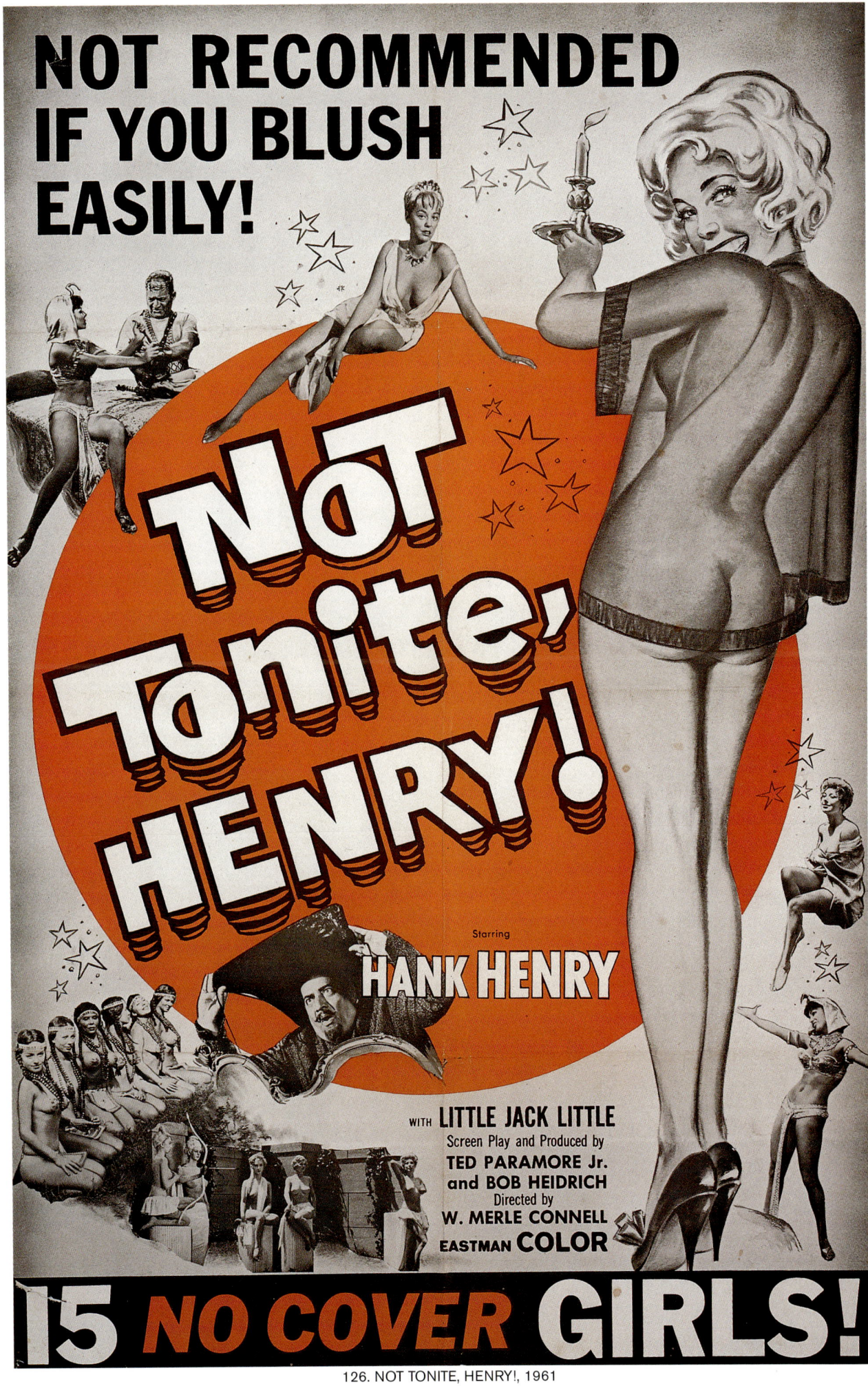

126. NOT TONITE, HENRY!, 1961

127. MA BARKER'S KILLER BROOD, 1960

128. BLUEBEARD'S 10 HONEYMOONS, 1960

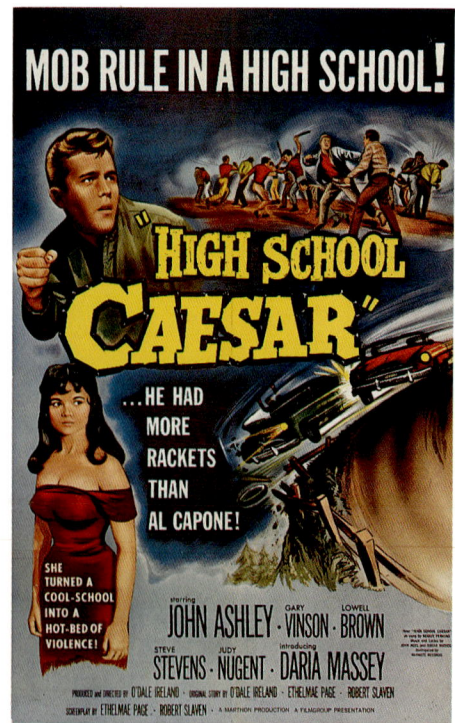
129. HIGH SCHOOL CAESAR, 1960

130. IT TAKES A THIEF, 1960

131. CIRCUS OF HORRORS, 1960

132. THE BELLBOY AND THE PLAYGIRLS, 1962

133. CONFESSIONS OF AN OPIUM EATER, 1962

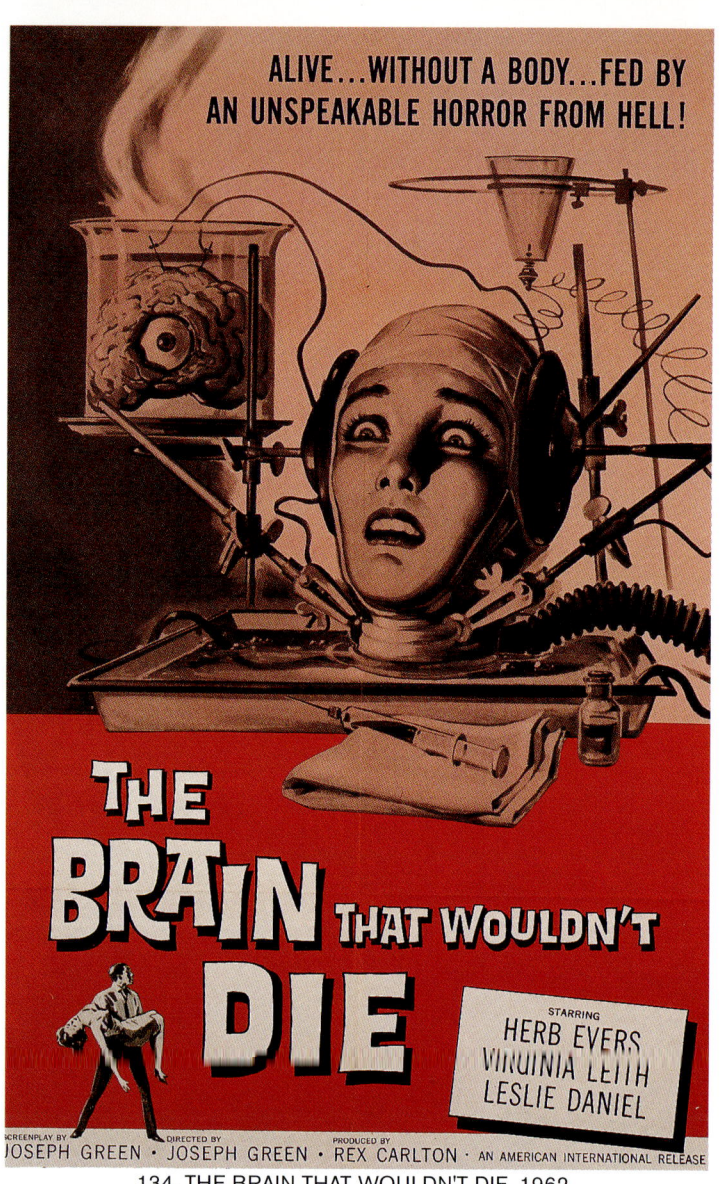
134. THE BRAIN THAT WOULDN'T DIE, 1962

135. KING KONG VS. GODZILLA, 1962

136. PANIC IN YEAR ZERO, 1962

137. HAND OF DEATH, 1962

138. SHOTGUN WEDDING, 1963

139. THE TERROR, 1963

140. BLOOD FEAST, 1963

141. THE INCREDIBLY STRANGE CREATURES WHO STOPPED LIVING AND BECAME MIXED-UP ZOMBIES, 1963

142. UNEARTHLY STRANGER, 1963

143. WEREWOLF IN A GIRLS' DORMITORY, 1963

150. BAD GIRLS GO TO HELL, 1965

151. THE BLACK KLANSMAN, 1966

152. THE WILD ANGELS, 1966

153. BILLY THE KID VS. DRACULA, 1966

154. LAS VEGAS HILLBILLYS, 1966

155. CONTEST GIRL, 1966

156. THE TRIP, 1967

157. LSD FLESH OF DEVIL, 1967, Italian poster

158. SOMETHING WEIRD, 1967

159. THE LOVE-INS, 1967

160. PSYCH-OUT, 1968

161. VIXEN, 1968

162. EVE, 1968

163. SPREE, 1967

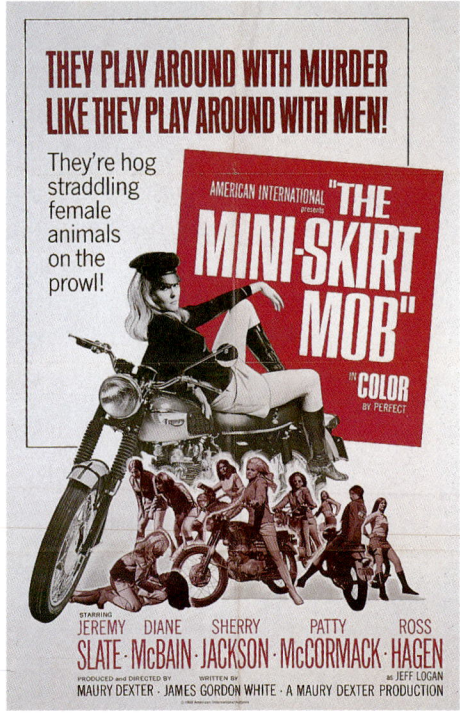
164. THE MINI-SKIRT MOB, 1968

165. BABY LOVE, 1968

166. NIGHT OF THE LIVING DEAD, 1968

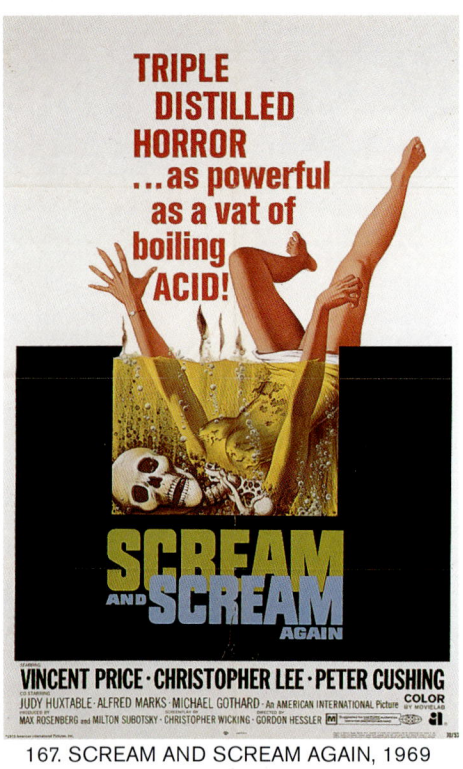
167. SCREAM AND SCREAM AGAIN, 1969

168. SCREAM BABY SCREAM, 1969

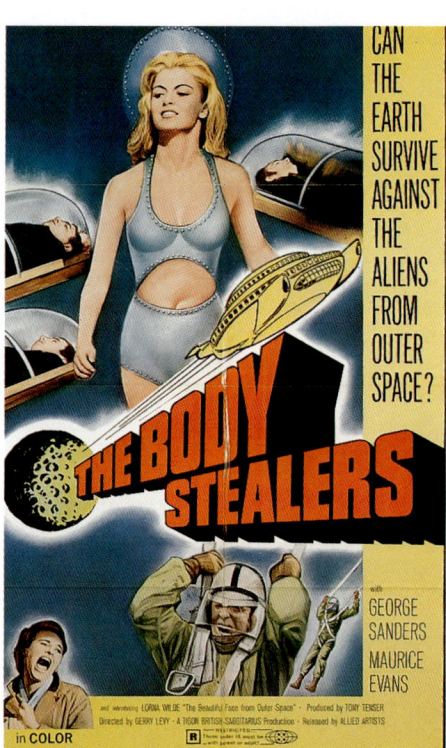
169. THE BODY STEALERS, 1969

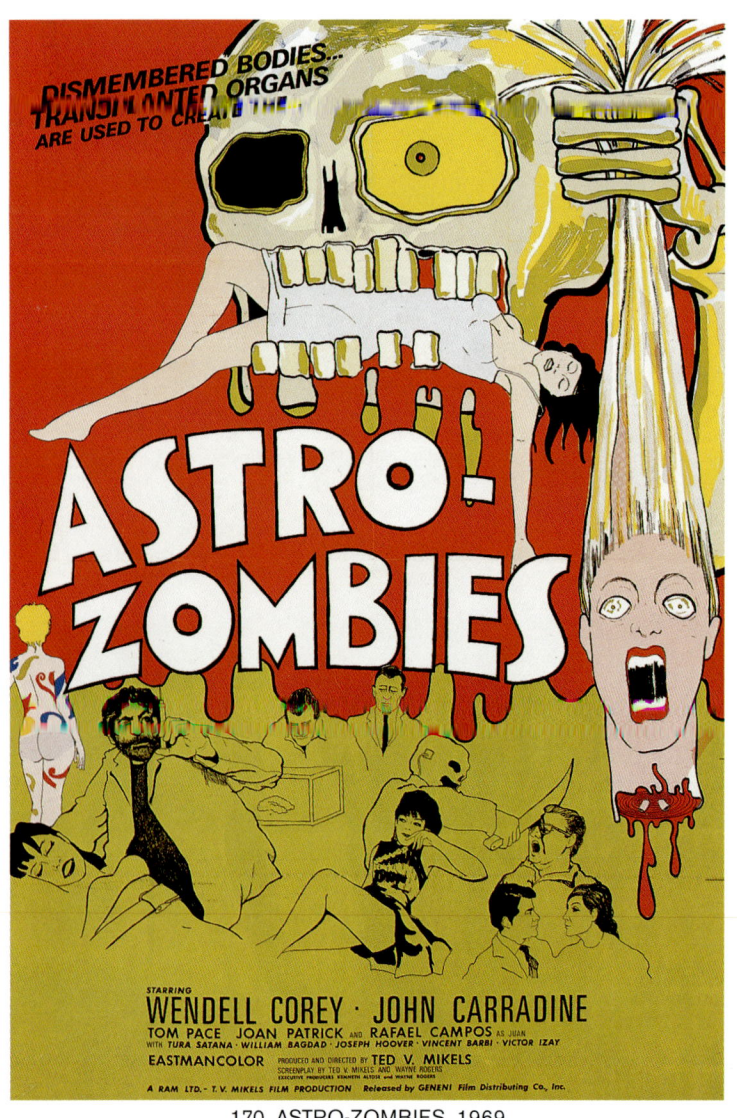
170. ASTRO-ZOMBIES, 1969

171. NIGHT OF BLOODY HORROR, 1969

172. EASY RIDER, 1969

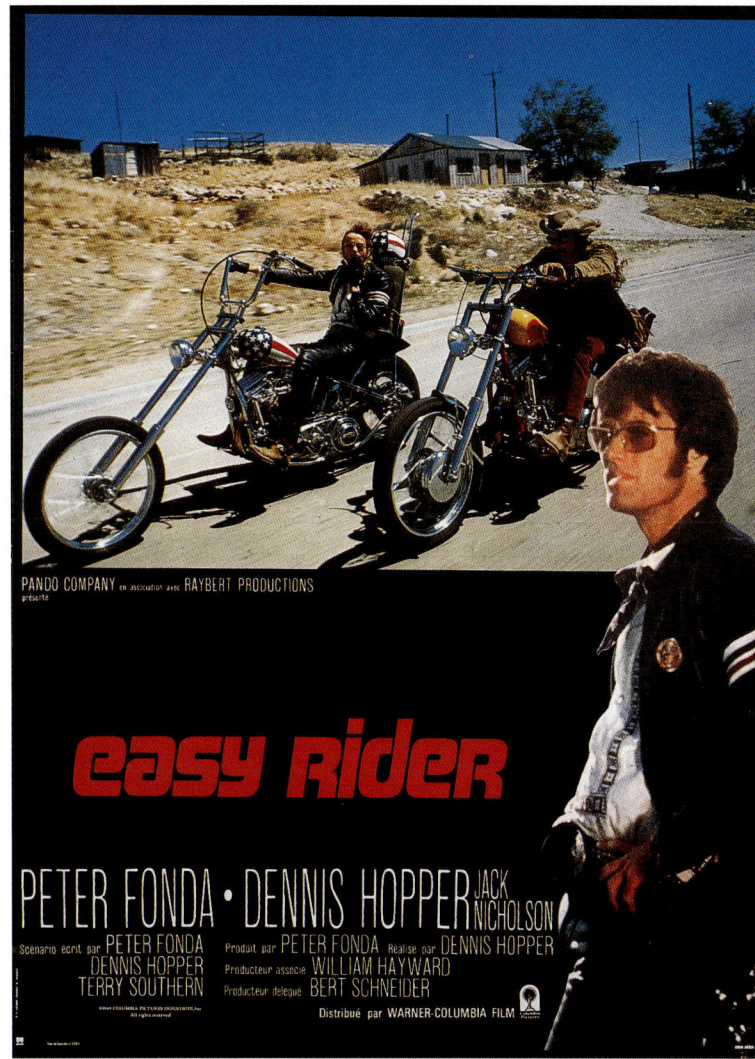
173. EASY RIDER, 1969, German poster

174. THE FEMALE BUNCH, 1969

175. NAKED ANGELS, 1969

176. THE CYCLE SAVAGES, 1969

177. THE LOVE FACTOR, 1969

178. CHERRY, HARRY & RAQUEL, 1969

179. CHASTITY, 1969

180. SCHOOL FOR UNCLAIMED GIRLS, 1969

181. WEDDING NIGHT, 1969

188. ANGELS HARD AS THEY COME, 1971

189. I AM A GROUPIE!, 1971

190. CHAIN GANG WOMEN, 1971

191. CHROME AND HOT LEATHER, 1971

192. WOMEN IN CAGES, 1971

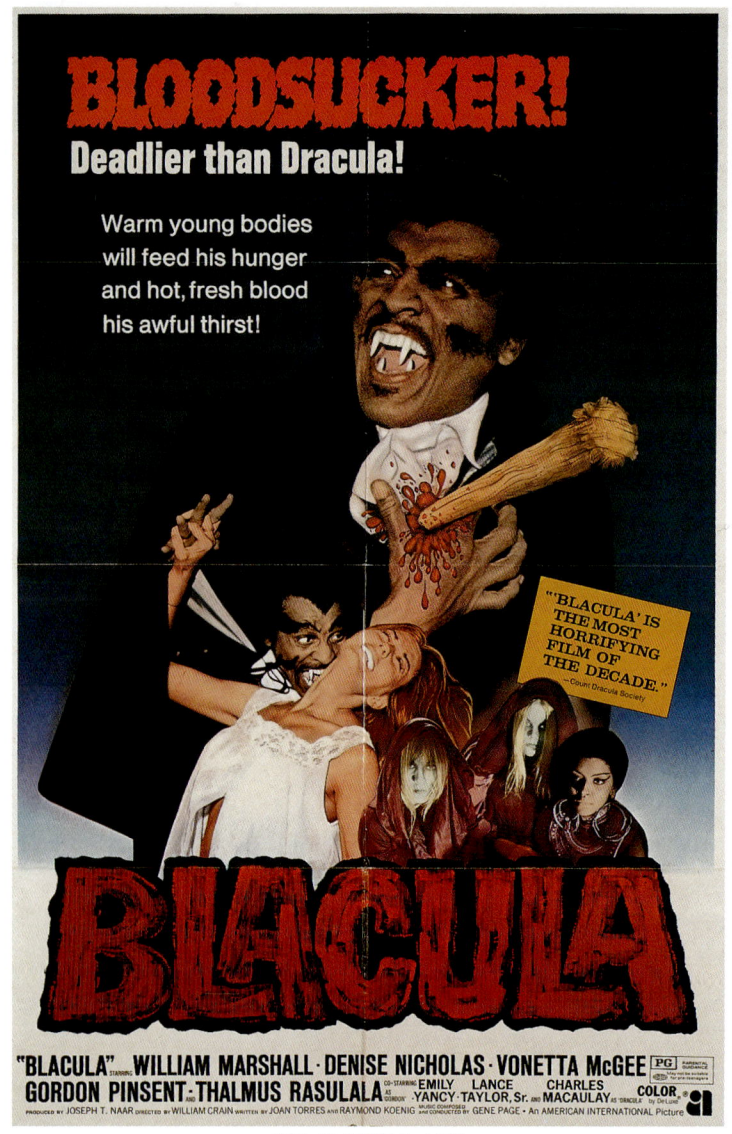
193. BLACULA, 1972

194. HIT MAN, 1972

195. SLAUGHTER, 1972

196. CLEOPATRA JONES, 1973

197. BLACK CAESAR, 1973

198. BLACK MAMA WHITE MAMA, 1972

199. THE HOT BOX, 1972

200. PICK UP ON 101, 1972

201. THE BIG BIRD CAGE, 1972

202. WOMEN IN CELL BLOCK 7, 1972

203. BOXCAR BERTHA, 1972

204. FROGS, 1972

205. ORGY OF THE LIVING DEAD, 1972

206. INVASION OF THE BLOOD FARMERS, 1972

207. THE WEREWOLF VS. VAMPIRE WOMAN, 1972

208. ASYLUM, 1972

209. LAST HOUSE ON THE LEFT, 1972

210. THE ARENA, 1973

211. SWEET SUZY, 1973

212. THE WORKING GIRLS, 1973

213. SEDUCE AND DESTROY, 1973

214. TEENAGE TRAMP, 1973

215. I DISMEMBER MAMA, 1974

216. THEY CALL HER ONE EYE, 1974

217. THE CARS THAT EAT PEOPLE, 1974

218. SNUFF, 1974

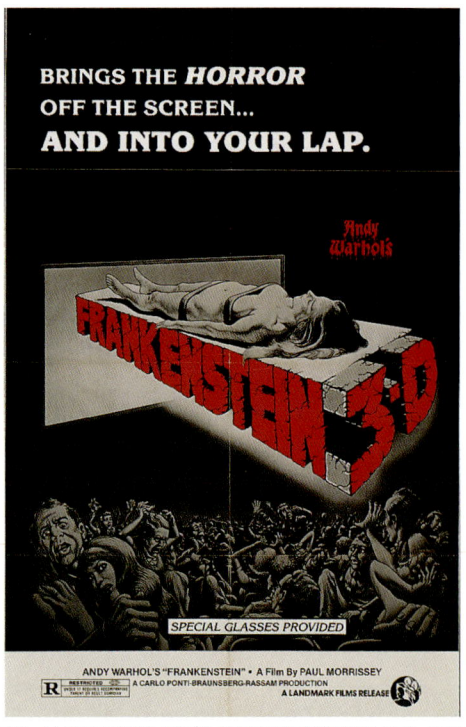
219. ANDY WARHOL'S FRANKENSTEIN 3-D, 1974

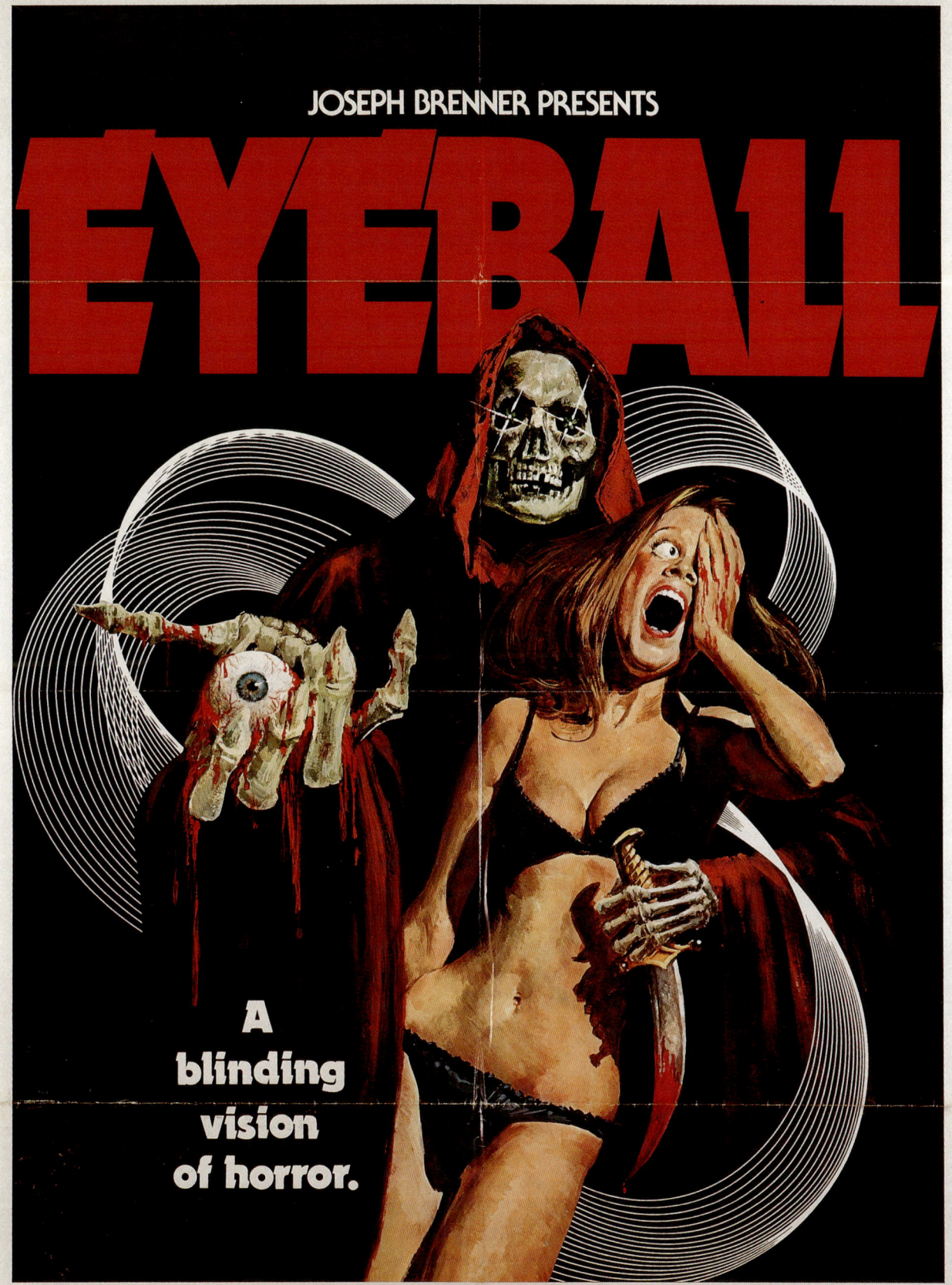

220. EYEBALL, 1974

221. TRUCK STOP WOMEN, 1974
222. CAGED HEAT, 1974
223. DIRTY O'NEILL THE LOVE LIFE OF A COP, 1974

224. SAVAGE SISTERS, 1974
225. MAMA'S DIRTY GIRLS, 1974

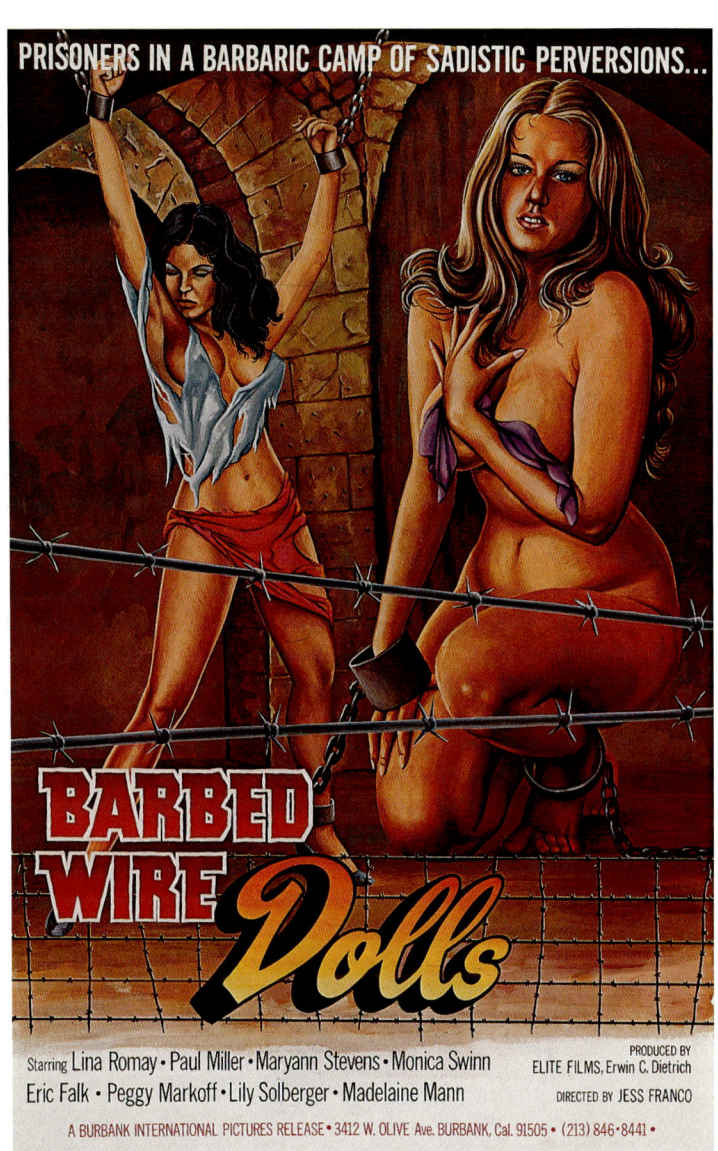

226. THE BOOB TUBE, 1975

227. BARBED WIRE DOLLS, 1975

228. SIX PACK ANNIE, 1975

229. SUPER VIXENS, 1975

230. CRAZY MAMA, 1975

231. TNT JACKSON, 1975

232. THE CANDY TANGERINE MAN, 1975

233. DR. BLACK MR. HYDE, 1976

234. FRIDAY FOSTER, 1975

235. THE BLACK GESTAPO, 1975

236. BLACK COBRA, 1976

237. TOMCATS, 1976

238. NAUGHTY SCHOOL GIRLS, 1976

239. SCHOOL DAYS, 1976

240. CHERRY HILL HIGH, 1976

241. SCORCHY, 1976

242. TOO HOT TO HANDLE, 1976

243. JACKSON COUNTY JAIL, 1976

244. 'GATOR BAIT, 1976

245. WOLF WOMAN, 1976

246. GOLIATHON, 1977

247. REVENGE OF THE SHOGUN WOMEN, 1977

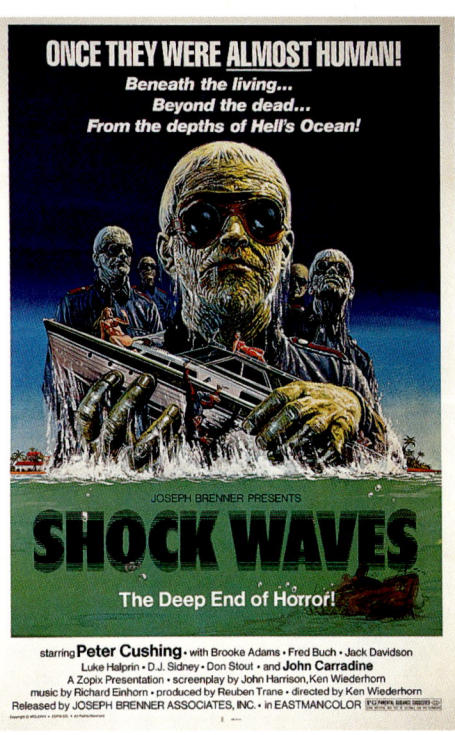

248. TINTOREA, 1977

249. NIGHT OF THE HOWLING BEAST, 1977

250. SHOCK WAVES, 1977

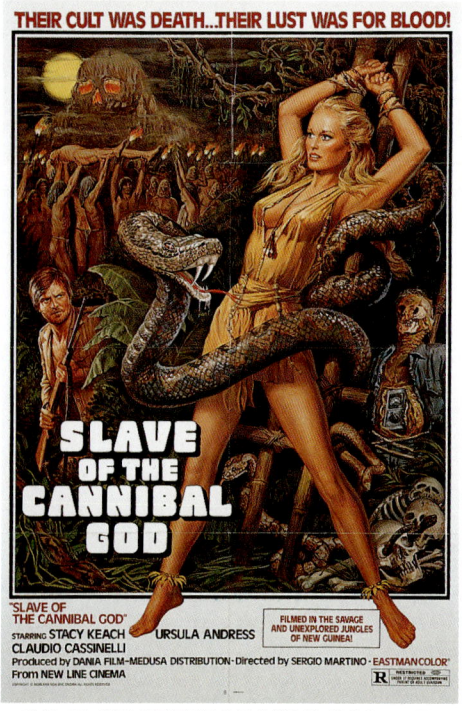

251. SLAVE OF THE CANNIBAL GOD, 1978

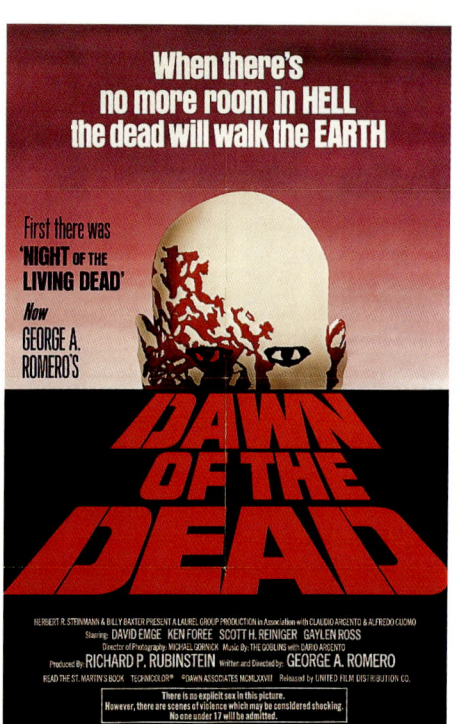

252. DAWN OF THE DEAD, 1978

253. MARDI GRAS MASSACRE, 1978

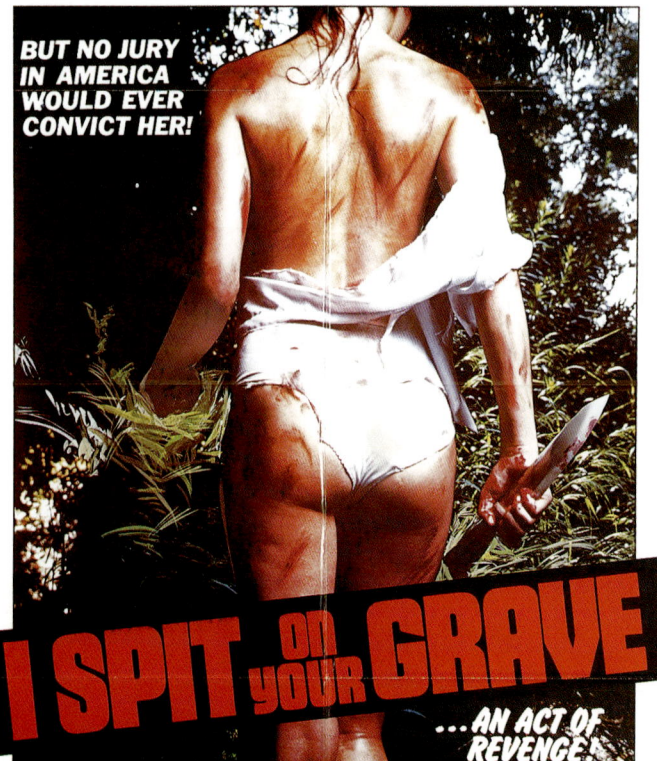

254. I SPIT ON YOUR GRAVE, 1978

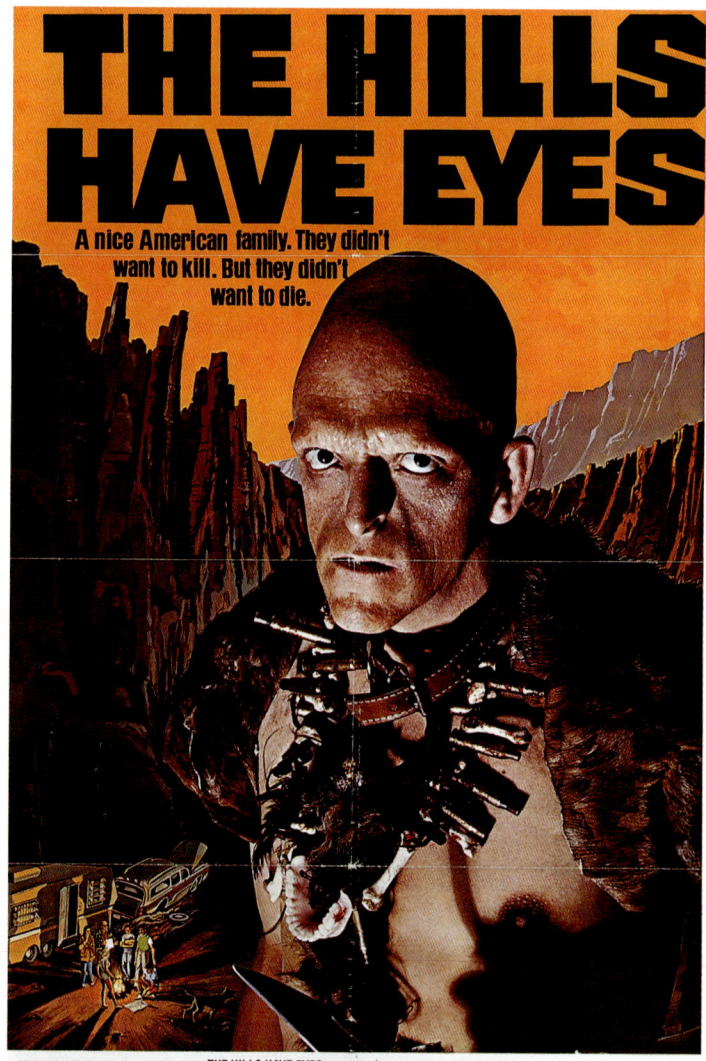

255. THE HILLS HAVE EYES, 1978

256. MOTEL HELL, 1980

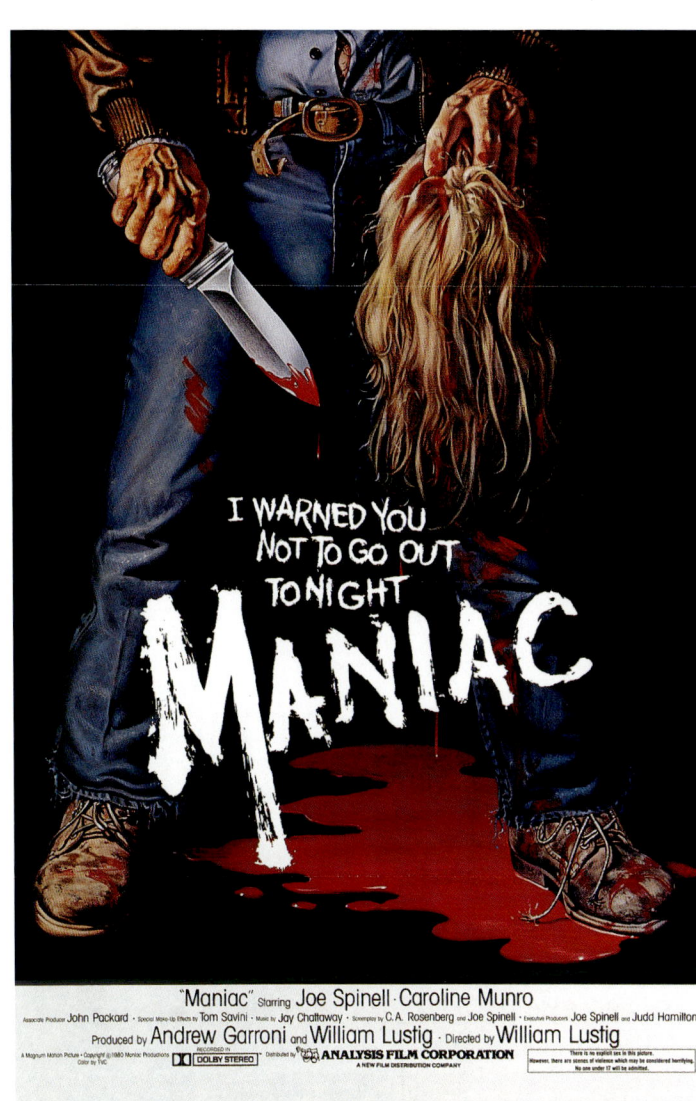
257. MANIAC, 1980

258. THE 7 BROTHERS MEET DRACULA, 1979

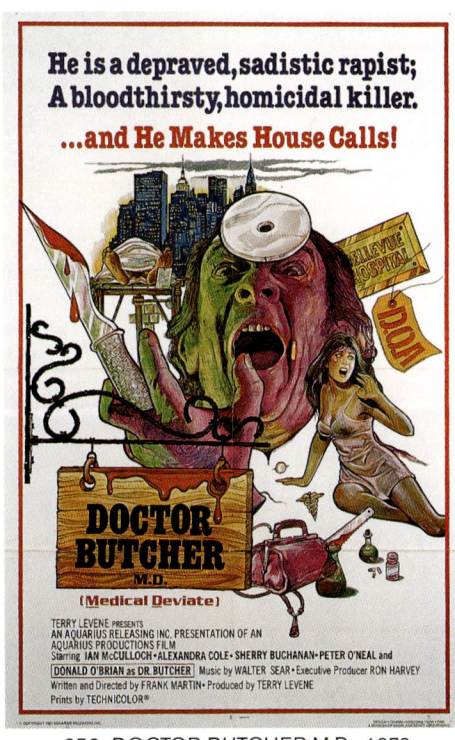
259. DOCTOR BUTCHER M.D., 1979

260. SORCERESS, 1980

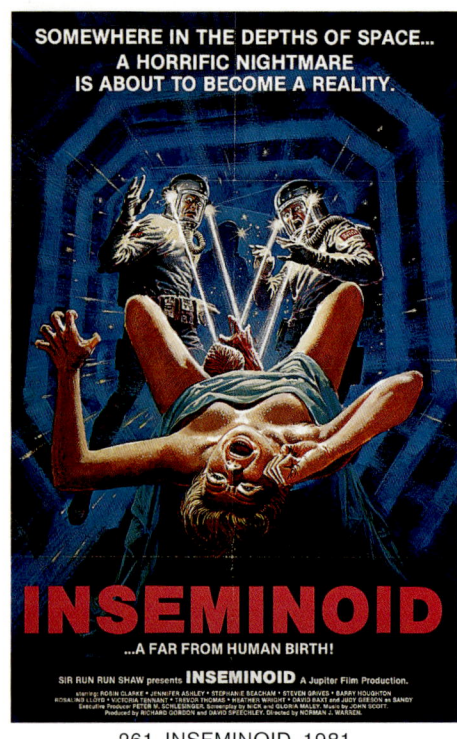
261. INSEMINOID, 1981

262. THE SLUMBER PARTY MASSACRE, 1982

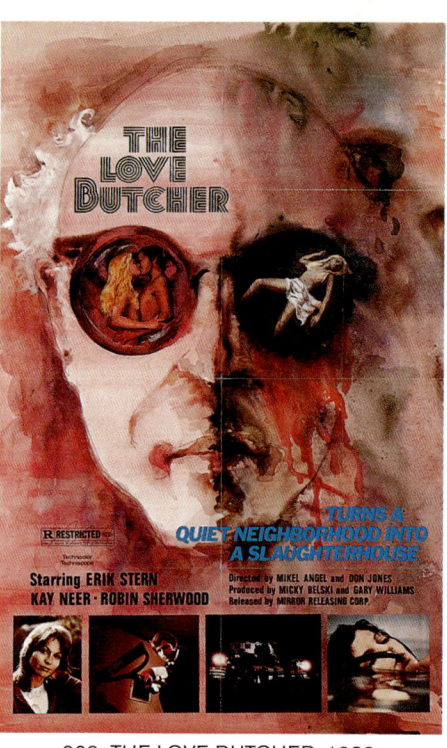
263. THE LOVE BUTCHER, 1982

264. MS. 45, 1981

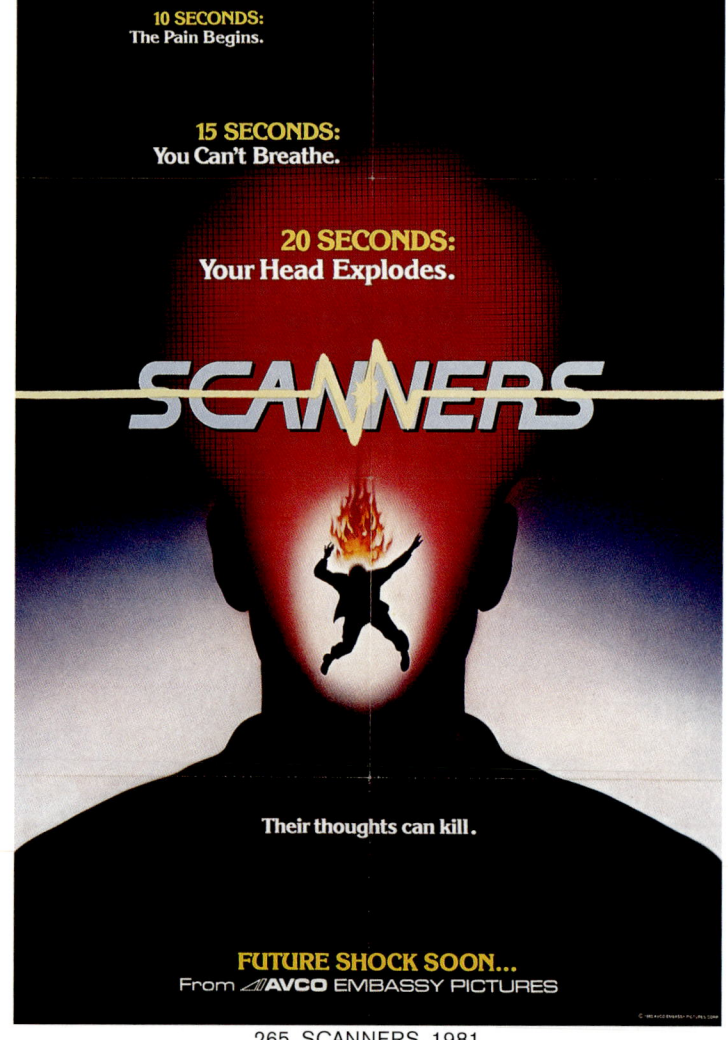
265. SCANNERS, 1981

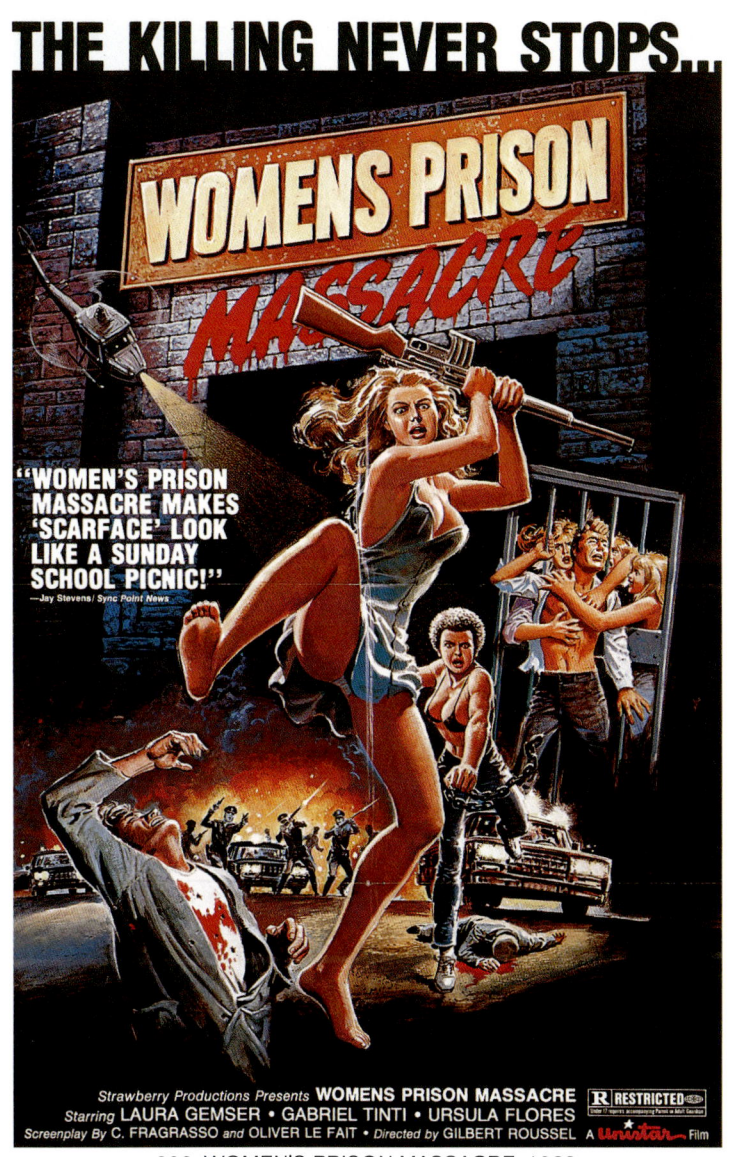

266. WOMEN'S PRISON MASSACRE, 1983

267. ZOMBIE ISLAND MASSACRE, 1984

268. THE HOUSE ON SORORITY ROW, 1983

269. CREEPERS, 1984

270. ANGEL, 1984

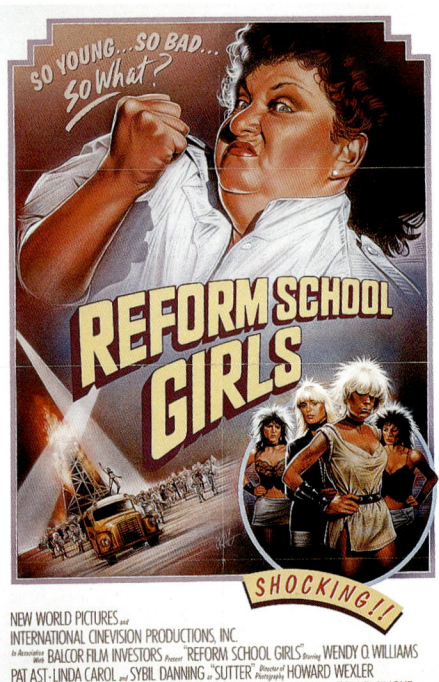
271. REFORM SCHOOL GIRLS, 1986

272. THE HITCHER, 1986

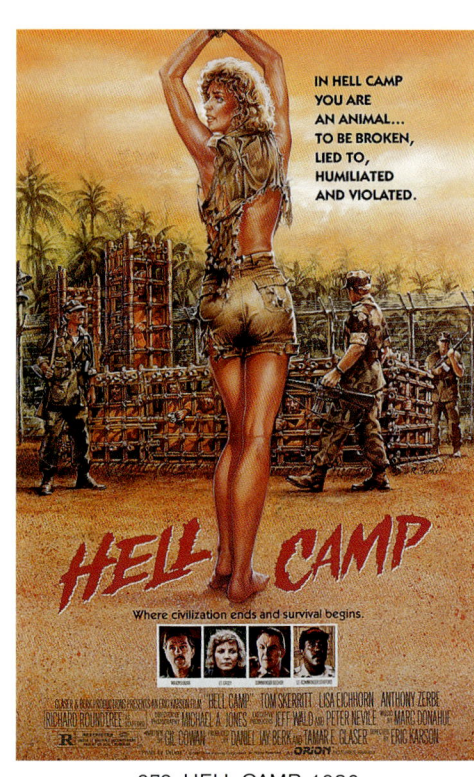
273. HELL CAMP, 1986

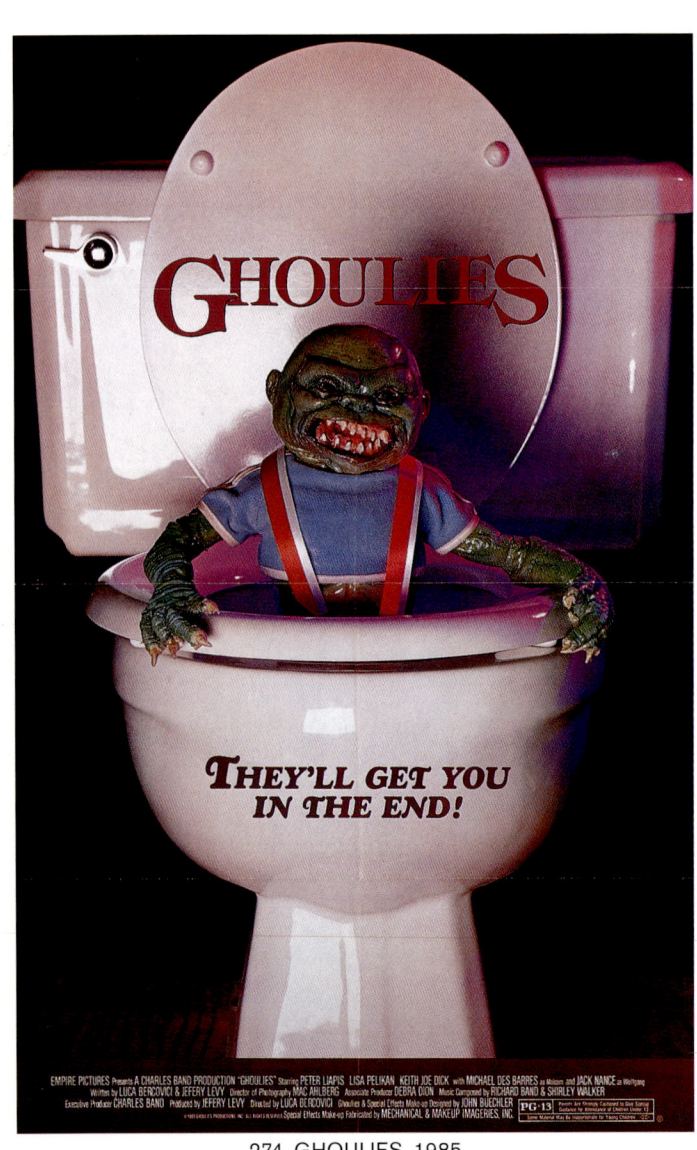
274. GHOULIES, 1985

275. WHITE SLAVE, 1986

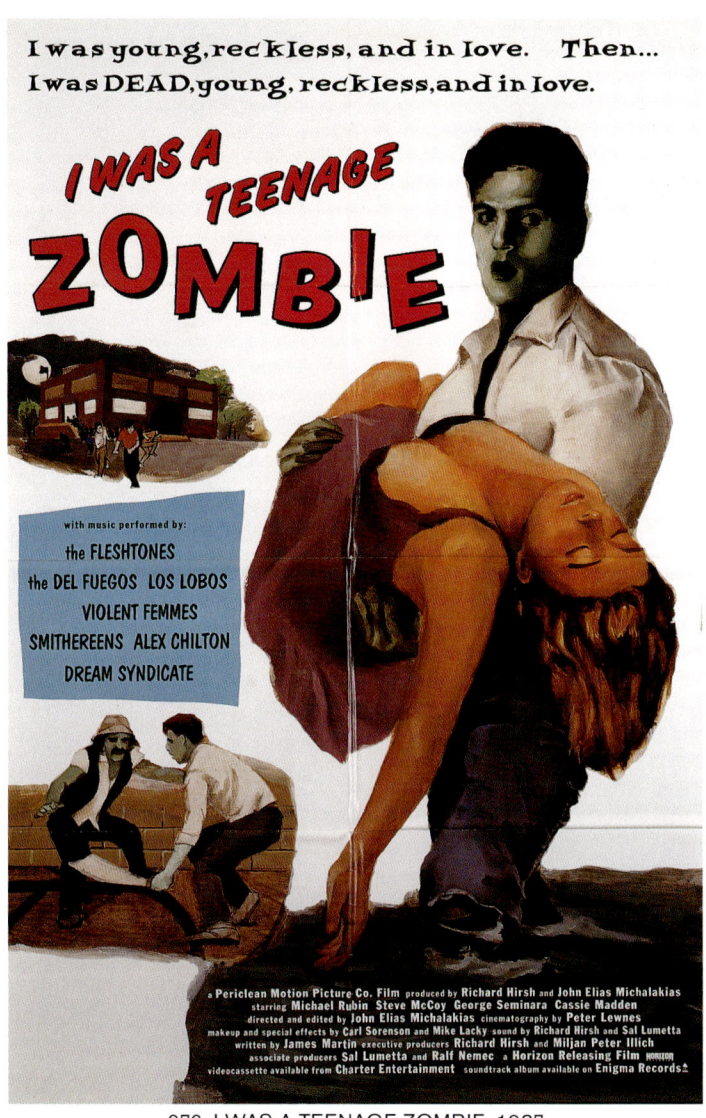

276. I WAS A TEENAGE ZOMBIE, 1987

277. SORORITY BABES IN THE SLIMEBALL BOWL-O-RAMA, 1988

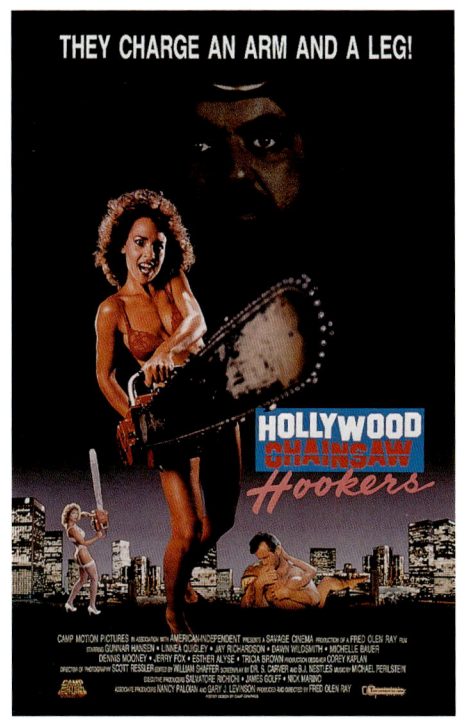

278. HOLLYWOOD CHAINSAW HOOKERS, 1988

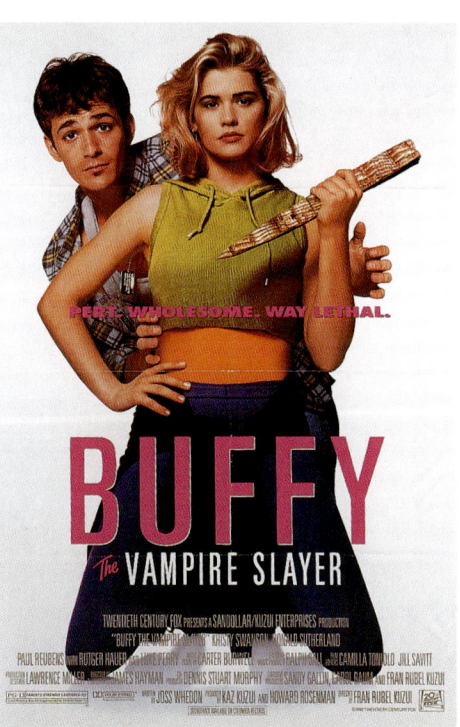

279. BUFFY THE VAMPIRE SLAYER, 1992

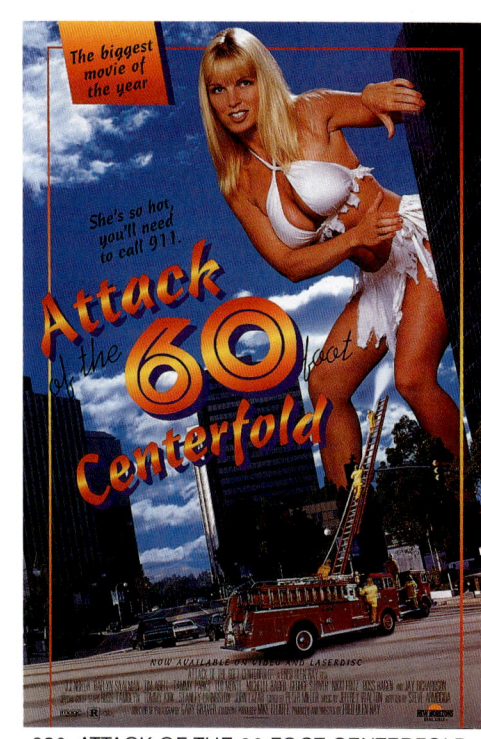

280. ATTACK OF THE 60 FOOT CENTERFOLD, 1996

ATTACK OF THE "B" MOVIE POSTERS INDEX

ANDY WARHOL'S FRANKENSTEIN 3-D	219
ANGEL	270
ANGELS HARD AS THEY COME	188
THE ARENA	210
ASSASSIN OF YOUTH	14
ASTRO-ZOMBIES	170
ASYLUM	208
ATTACK OF THE 60 FOOT CENTERFOLD	280
ATTACK OF THE 50 FT. WOMAN	106
BABY LOVE	165
BACK FROM THE DEAD	85
BAD GIRL	3
BAD GIRLS GO TO HELL	150
BARBED WIRE DOLLS	227
BELA LUGOSI MEETS A BROOKLYN GORILLA	51
THE BELLBOY AND THE PLAYGIRLS	132
THE BIG BIRD CAGE	201
BILLY THE KID VS. DRACULA	153
BLACK CAESAR	197
BLACK COBRA	236
THE BLACK GESTAPO	235
THE BLACK KLANSMAN	151
BLACK MAMA WHITE MAMA	198
BLACULA	193
BLAZE STARR GOES NUDIST	118
BLOOD FEAST	140
BLOOD LUST/BLOOD MANIA	187
BLOOD MANIA	186
BLUEBEARD'S 10 HONEYMOONS	128
THE BODY STEALERS	169
THE BONNIE PARKER STORY	104
THE BOOB TUBE	226
BORN TO BE BAD	5
BOXCAR BERTHA	203
THE BRAIN EATERS	95
THE BRAIN THAT WOULDN'T DIE	134
THE BRIDE AND THE BEAST	93
A BUCKET OF BLOOD	108
THE BUCKSKIN LADY	64
BUFFY THE VAMPIRE SLAYER	279
THE BURNING QUESTION	13
CAGED HEAT	222
THE CANDY TANGERINE MAN	232
CAPTIVE WILD WOMAN	21
THE CARS THAT EAT PEOPLE	217
THE CAT GIRL	83
CAT-WOMAN OF THE MOON	49
CHAIN GANG WOMEN	190
CHASTITY	179
CHERRY HILL HIGH	240
CHERRY, HARRY & RAQUEL	178
CHILDREN OF THE WILD	22
CHROME AND HOT LEATHER	191
CIRCUS OF HORRORS	131
CLEOPATRA JONES	196
COD AND THE CRAZY	101
COME DANCE WITH ME!	114
CONFESSIONS OF AN OPIUM EATER	133
CONTEST GIRL	155
THE COSMIC MAN	107
THE CRAWLING EYE	94
CRAZY MAMA	230
CREEPERS	269
THE CYCLE SAVAGES	176
THE CYCLOPS	84
DATE BAIT	117
DAWN OF THE DEAD	252
DEVIL'S HARVEST	16
DEVIL'S HARVEST	17
DIRTY O'NEILL THE LOVE LIFE OF A COP	223
DOCTOR BUTCHER M.D.	259
DR. BLACK MR. HYDE	233
DRAGSTRIP GIRL	77
EASY RIDER	173
EASY RIDER	172
EVE	162
EVERYBODY'S GIRL	32
EYEBALL	220
FASTER, PUSSYCAT! KILL! KILL!	144
FEMALE AND THE FLESH	59
THE FEMALE BUNCH	174
FIVE BLOODY GRAVES	183
FLAMING YOUTH	1
FLESH FEAST	184
THE FLESH IS WEAK/BLONDE IN BONDAGE	72
FRANKENSTEIN	88
FRIDAY FOSTER	234
FROGS	204
GAMBLING WITH SOULS	9
'GATOR BAIT	244
GHOULIES	274
THE GIANT GILA MONSTER	109
THE GIANT LEECHES	124
GIRL WITH AN ITCH	74
GIRLS IN CHAINS	24
GIRLS IN PRISON	73
GIRLS ON THE LOOSE	105
GIRLS UNDER 21	19
GOLIATHON	246
GUN CRAZY	40
GUNS GIRLS AND GANGSTERS	110
HAND OF DEATH	137
THE HAUNTED STRANGLER	96
HELL CAMP	273
HIGH SCHOOL CAESAR	129
HIGH SCHOOL CONFIDENTIAL	100
HIGH SCHOOL HELLCATS	98
THE HILLS HAVE EYES	255
HIT MAN	194
THE HITCHER	272
HOLLYWOOD CHAINSAW HOOKERS	278
THE HOT BOX	199
HOT CAR GIRL	78
HOT MONEY GIRL	113
HOT ROD GANG	79
HOT ROD RUMBLE	76
HOUSE ON HAUNTED HILL	90
THE HOUSE ON SORORITY ROW	268
HOW TO MAKE A MONSTER	89
THE HYPNOTIC EYE	125
I AM A GROUPIE!	189
I BURY THE LIVING	92
I DISMEMBER MAMA	215
I LOVE TROUBLE	39
I PASSED FOR WHITE	116
I SPIT ON YOUR GRAVE	254
I WALK ALONE	34
I WAS A SHOPLIFTER	42
I WAS A TEENAGE FRANKENSTEIN	70
I WAS A TEENAGE ZOMBIE	276
THE INCREDIBLY STRANGE CREATURES WHO STOPPED LIVING AND BECAME MIXED-UP ZOMBIES	141
INSEMINOID	261
INVASION OF THE BLOOD FARMERS	206
IT TAKES A THIEF	130
JACKSON COUNTY JAIL	243
JESSE JAMES' WOMEN	61
JUKE JOINT	29
JUNGLE HEADHUNTERS	50
KILL OR BE KILLED	41
KING KONG VS. GODZILLA	135
LAS VEGAS HILLBILLYS	154
LAST HOUSE ON THE LEFT	209
THE LAST WOMAN ON EARTH	122
LIVE FAST, DIE YOUNG	102
LORNA	145
LOST LONELY AND VICIOUS	99
THE LOVE BUTCHER	263
THE LOVE FACTOR	177
THE LOVE WANGA	10
THE LOVE-INS	159
LSD FLESH OF DEVIL	157
MA BARKER'S KILLER BROOD	127
MACUMBA LOVE	123
MAMA'S DIRTY GIRLS	225
THE MAN FROM PLANET X	44
MANIAC	257
MARDI GRAS MASSACRE	253
MARIHUANA	15
THE MINI-SKIRT MOB	164
MONSTER FROM THE OCEAN FLOOR	48
MOONSHINE MOUNTAIN	147
MOTEL HELL	256
MOTORPSYCHO	146
MS. 45	264
MURDER BY TELEVISION	6
NAKED ANGELS	175
NAUGHTY BUT NICE	18
NAUGHTY SCHOOL GIRLS	238
THE NEANDERTHAL MAN	53
NIGHT OF BLOODY HORROR	171
NIGHT OF THE HOWLING BEAST	249
NIGHT OF THE LIVING DEAD	166
THE NIGHT RUNNER	71
NIGHT WAITRESS	7
NOT OF THIS EARTH	69
NOT TONITE, HENRY!	126
ONE GIRL'S CONFESSION	54
21,000 CONVICTS AND A WOMAN	18
ORDERED TO LOVE	120
ORGY OF THE LIVING DEAD	205
OUTLAW WOMEN	60
PANIC IN YEAR ZERO	136
PEEPING TOM	119
PICK UP ON 101	200
PICKUP1	43
PICKUP ALLEY	75
PITFALLS OF PASSION	2
PLAN 9 FROM OUTER SPACE	82
PLAYGIRL AFTER DARK	112
PORT SINISTER	47
PRISON WITHOUT BARS	12
PSYCH-OUT	160
QUEEN OF OUTER SPACE	91
RAMROD	36
RAT FINK	148
REFORM SCHOOL GIRL	65
REFORM SCHOOL GIRLS	271
THE RESTLESS BREED	62
RETURN OF THE FLY	97
REVENGE OF THE SHOGUN WOMEN	247
ROAD GANG	8
ROAD RACERS	80
ROBOT MONSTER	45
ROCK ALL NIGHT	56
ROCK, PRETTY BABY!	55
ROCK, ROCK, ROCK!	58
ROUGHSHOD	38
SAVAGE SISTERS	224
SCANNERS	265
SCHOOL DAYS	239
SCHOOL FOR UNCLAIMED GIRLS	180
SCORCHY	241
SCREAM AND SCREAM AGAIN	167
SCREAM BABY SCREAM	168
SEDUCE AND DESTROY	213
THE 7 BROTHERS MEET DRACULA	258
SHAKE, RATTLE AND ROCK	57
SHE DEMONS	87
THE SHE-CREATURE	66
SHOCK WAVES	250
SHOTGUN WEDDING	138
SHOULD A GIRL SAY YES?	30
THE SIN OF NORA MORAN	4
SIX PACK ANNIE	228
SLAUGHTER	195
SLAVE OF THE CANNIBAL GOD	251
THE SLUMBER PARTY MASSACRE	262
SNUFF	218
SO YOUNG, SO BAD	33
SOMETHING WEIRD	158
SON OF BELLE STARR	63
SORCERESS	260
SORORITY BABES IN THE SLIMEBALL BOWL-O-RAMA	277
SPEED CRAZY	81
SPREE	163
SUPER VIXENS	229
SWEET SUZY	211
TEEN AGE	25
TEEN AGE	26
TEENAGE MOTHER	149
TEENAGE TRAMP	214
THE TERROR	139
TERROR FROM THE YEAR 5,000	86
THEY CALL HER ONE EYE	216
THEY LIVE BY NIGHT	35
TINTOREA	248
TNT JACKSON	231
TOMCATS	237
TOO HOT TO HANDLE	242
TOO LATE FOR TEARS	37
TORMENTED	121
THE TRIP	156
TRUCK STOP WOMEN	221
20 MILLION MILES TO EARTH	67
UNDER AGE	20
THE UNEARTHLY	68
UNEARTHLY STRANGE	142
UNTAMED MISTRESS	52
VICE RAID	115
VIRGIN SACRIFICE	111
VIXEN	161
THE WAGES OF SIN	11
WEDDING NIGHT	181
WEREWOLF IN A GIRLS' DORMITORY	143
THE WEREWOLF VS. VAMPIRE WOMAN	207
WHEN DINOSAURS RULED THE EARTH	185
WHITE SLAVE	275
WHY GIRLS LEAVE HOME	28
THE WILD ANGELS	152
WOLF WOMAN	245
WOMEN IN CAGES	192
WOMEN IN CELL BLOCK 7	202
WOMEN'S PRISON MASSACRE	266
THE WORKING GIRLS	212
YOUNG AND WILD	103
YOUNG WIDOW	31
YOUTH AFLAME	27
YOUTH RUNS WILD	23
ZOMBIE ISLAND MASSACRE	267
ZOMBIES OF THE STRATOSPHERE	46